A Border Beat

Policing in Dundalk

Pat O'Donoghue

First Edition
Published 2020

© 2020 Pat O'Donoghue

Pat O'Donoghue asserts his right to the intellectual property contained in this work
All rights reserved.

No part of this book may be reproduced or used in any form or by any means digital, electronic or mechanical including but not confined to photography filming video recording photocopying or by any information storage and retrieval system existing or in the future to be devised and shall not by way of trade or otherwise be lent resold or otherwise circulated in any form of binding or cover other than that in which it is published without prior permission in writing from the publishers.

ISBN 978-1-908784-08-7

British Library Cataloguing in Publication Data

A catalogue record for this book is available from the British Library
The publishers have made every reasonable effort to contact the copyright holders of photographs and texts reproduced in this book. If any involuntary infringement of copyright has occurred, sincere apologies are offered and the owners of such copyright are requested to contact the
publishers

Printed and Bound by Dundalk Bookbinding

I dedicate this book
to the memory of
the five Gardaí who lost their lives
in the course of their duty
in Dundalk Garda District.

Garda John Lally
Sergeant Patrick Morrissey
Detective Garda Desmond Dixon
Detective Garda Adrian Donohoe
Garda Tony Golden

Acknowledgements

Having been based in Dundalk Garda district since the mid-1970s I was lucky enough in my early years to have made the acquaintance of local photographer Paul Kavanagh (a Garda's son), who encouraged me to gather up old police and Garda photographs of the area and retain them. He himself had taken many Garda photographs and entrusted them to me. With his assistance and encouragement, I contacted the Garda museum, and with the help of Sergeant John Duffy and Pauline Duffy, I acquired more material, so that by the time of the 75th anniversary of the force, I was in a position to produce a commemorative booklet.

By this stage my collection was getting bigger and more interesting. I had worked through some of the most challenging times of Dundalk's policing history and I felt this notable time had to be recorded. After retiring in 2005 I continued gathering information and in 2014 I was approached by Michael Gaynor, chairperson of the Old Dundalk Society, to give a talk on Policing in Dundalk. After that, I decided to collate all my stories and photographs and publish them.

Initially I contacted Liam McNiffe, author of *A History of an Garda Síochána* and asked him for advice and guidance. Liam gave me the encouragement I needed to start writing and I remember his parting shot to me, "Pat, write it your way, you lived it".

Thus the book had begun and so had the testing of my friends' and especially my wife's patience. Unaccustomed as I was to writing, this proved challenging until I got invaluable guidance and assistance from my good friend and neighbour Trevor Patterson.

I especially wish to thank retired Detective Garda Michael O'Driscoll who assisted me greatly in the research of the Scott Medallists and the many other Gardaí and their families who contributed greatly to this publication. I would also like to acknowledge the Morrissey, Holland, Henry and Wymes families who gave me access to family records. I wish to give thanks to Louth County Archivist Lorraine McCann, Jimmy Bellew, Victor Whitmarsh, Noel Ross, Stephen O'Donnell, Pat Mulligan, Brendan Flynn, Brendan McAvinue, Army Sergeant Ricardo Lucchesi, the Duggan family and Harriet Andrews. I wish to express my gratitude to all the people who supplied me with photographs, especially Paula Kavanagh who allowed me to publish photographs from the Paul Kavanagh Collection which can be accessed on-line at www.pkphotography.ie. Last but not least a special thank you to my dear wife Liz for all the support and the help she gave me during this crusade.

I wish to thank the following sponsors for their generosity.
Their financial support was greatly appreciated and made it possible
for the publication of this book.

Martin Naughton *Glen Dimplex Group*
Larry Goodman *ABP Food Group*
Dundalk Credit Union
Mary McCann *Fyffes*
St Raphael's Garda Credit Union, Dublin
Frank Lynch & Co Chartered Certified Accountants
Garda Representative Association

The proceeds from this book are being donated to Dundalk Simon Community
and Woman's Aid Dundalk.

Contents

Foreword		8
Chapter 1	Introduction	9
Chapter 2	Policing before 1922	11
Chapter 3	1922 to 1970	21
Chapter 4	1970s	37
Chapter 5	1980s	47
Chapter 6	1990s onwards	54
Chapter 7	History of Dundalk Garda Station	66
Chapter 8	Local Garda Commissioners	71
Conclusion		72
Addendum		73
Bibliography		76

Foreword

On this island, a generation has grown up since the violence and heartbreak of the so-called "Troubles" were brought to a close. Most of those now in their early thirties would have little or no concept of the tit-for-tat killings, the assassinations, the car bombs, the disappeared, those speeches calling for peace and those inciting hatred and violence. They have never had to suffer the inconvenience of the permanent security checkpoints on main roads in Northern Ireland nor the impromptu Garda checkpoints set up to combat the violence and lawlessness that was criss-crossing the border. Even younger members of the Garda Síochána would be hard put to visualise how the force, over a period of three decades and particularly in border districts, had to confront the threats posed by those who used the bomb and the bullet rather than dialogue towards achieving their aims. Even to this day the effects of that period can still be felt as a form of inherited lawlessness is often displayed.

Pat O'Donoghue has lived all his life on the border and his Garda career has spanned most of the period of the Troubles, including thirty years serving in Dundalk District. Because of its geographical location as a large industrial town some few miles from South Down and South Armagh, and mid-way between Belfast and Dublin, Dundalk was impacted more by those events in Northern Ireland than anywhere else south of the border. Consequently, the duties of members of the Garda Síochána in that district were often "unusually demanding" and resulted in "truly courageous responses" and tragedies.

O'Donoghue's research also covers the earlier policing of Dundalk including, in 1922, the replacement of the RIC by the Civic Guard and how the renamed, unarmed, and inexperienced Garda Síochána evolved through the growing pains of the Irish Free State and, latterly, the Irish Republic. He draws on his personal memories and experiences and those of former colleagues to describe a catalogue of incidents, often violent and sometimes tragic within the district between the early 1970s and 2015. The book, well-illustrated, is a fitting tribute to the bravery and integrity of the members of the Garda Síochána within Dundalk District, particularly those who forfeited their lives in the protection of peace.

Brendan McAvinue

Brendan McAvinue is a graduate of the extra-mural certificate course in local history at NUI Maynooth. He is the grandson of Civic Guard number two, who also served as a member of the Royal Irish Constabulary. He has written and lectured on the history of policing in Co. Louth.

Chapter 1

- Introduction -

The evening of 21st September 1972 was to be a defining moment in the policing history of Dundalk and its townspeople. An event occurred that was to have far reaching consequences for Gardaí and the security of the State. Up to that evening local Gardaí policed Dundalk in a similar manner to any other large provincial town in Ireland.

At around 6 pm a political protest rally took place at the Market Square with about a hundred people in attendance. At the end of the rally a man with a loudspeaker called on the crowd to line up in military formation and march to the Garda Station at the Crescent. On their way to the Station they ripped up paving stones for ammunition. A lorry was also hijacked to block the road. Groups of local youths were enticed to join the mob and willingly did so. By the time they reached the Garda Station their numbers had swollen to about two hundred. They then proceeded to attack the Station with stones and petrol bombs.

Sergeant Hugh Shreenan was the Station Sergeant at the time and he, his wife and two year old daughter lived in the married quarters. On this evening he was there with his family and a small number of Gardaí when the attack took place.

Very soon the rioters had broken all the front windows of the Garda Station, and a patrol car and private members' cars had been overturned and burned. The mob then proceeded to break in the front door of the station. The situation at this stage was terrifying. Severe danger and possible loss of life were imminent were it not for the quick thinking and bravery of Detective Garda Denis Daly who managed to get his hands on an official machine gun, faced the mob, and fired volleys of shots over their heads. The sound of gunfire scattered the mob from the front of the station.

Earlier, phone calls for assistance had been made to outlying Garda stations and the local army barracks. Troops from the 27th Battalion in full riot gear were first to arrive on the scene. The rioters confronted them and pelted them with stones and pavings, and eventually the troops had to fire CS gas to gain control. At the same time a fire engine trying to make its way to the Garda Station also came under attack, with its windows and equipment being smashed. Fire brigade assistance was also summoned from Drogheda and Carrickmacross. As the rioters made their way back to the town centre, the army ringed the Garda Barracks for fear of further attacks.

On their way to the town centre the mob ran riot, breaking traffic lights and shop windows while looting and creating as much mayhem as they possibly could. By this stage extra Gardaí had arrived on the scene from nearby stations and faced the rioters at the Market Square. The sight of the Gardaí approaching with their batons drawn was enough to make the rioters disperse and run up side streets. The town eventually became saturated with Gardaí resulting, after a time, with law and order being restored.

The following morning showed serious scars of a night's rioting. Since the foundation of the State this was the first time a Garda Station was attacked in such a manner with such devastating consequences for the town it was protecting. Questions were to be asked and answered. As it turned out, it was to be an indicator or a wakeup call for the authorities of an emerging very dangerous era.

With the spillover of the northern conflict, the next twenty to thirty years were to be a severe testing time for every city, town and village countrywide. But Dundalk Garda District, due its geographical position, would be tested more than most. For within the district, since the beginning of the 1970s, three members of An Garda Síochána were murdered on duty; over twenty Scott medals were awarded to Gardaí for facing down gunfire and other acts of bravery; and, unfortunately, two other members were accidentally killed on duty. The town was bombed and atrocious murders took place.

However, before exploring policing in this violent period, it is worth examining how policing evolved in Dundalk and its hinterland. Prior this watershed event at Dundalk Garda Station in 1972, Dundalk already had a history reaching back over a century and a half, since the first formal police service was introduced to Co Louth in 1816.

Chapter 2
- Policing before 1922 -

When Sir Robert Peel became Irish Home Secretary in 1812 he saw the need to address the agrarian trouble in rural Ireland and decided something had to be done. Prior to the 19th century the British Government normally tried to keep order in Ireland with either militias or regular soldiers, but it was expensive to station enough soldiers throughout the country, and besides these soldiers would shortly be needed in Europe to meet the final challenge of the French army under Napoleon Bonaparte. It was also recognised that policing duties were not good for military discipline, as it amounted to asking men who might be fighting Napoleon one year to look for illicit stills in the Irish countryside the next. Urban policing at the time was also performed by the night watchmen or part-time policemen appointed by local authorities such as the Grand Jury. These appointees had next to no training and were very poorly paid.

A new structured system of policing was established in Ireland by Sir Robert Peel's Peace Preservation Act of 1814 and this was to be the forerunner of modern day policing. The Peace Preservation Act provided for a Peace Preservation Force which was not a permanently stationed police force, but instead a unit which could be deployed in an area which was particularly disturbed. As most of County Louth was experiencing agrarian violence early in 1816, a force of 100 men was sent to the county. Along with Tipperary, Clare and Cavan, Louth was one of the first counties to experience the use of the Peace Preservation Force.

This arrangement was followed some years later with the passing of the Constabulary Act on 5th August 1822 which laid the basis for the first permanent country-wide police force. This act established four provincial police forces with depots in the North (Armagh), West (Ballinrobe), Midlands (Daingean) and South (Ballincollig), centrally administered from Dublin Castle, and the police were known as the County Constabulary. Applicants for this new force had to be able to read and write and be of good character. They were paid up to £30 per year and were supplied with a proper uniform. They received three months training at their provincial headquarters and then, armed with short flintlock carbines, were sent to their respective stations.

The next major change in Irish policing came under the stewardship of Thomas Drummond, who was Under Secretary for Ireland from 1835 up to his death in 1840. Born a Scotsman in Edinburgh, he is reputed to have had a great and true understanding of the Irish and their grievances. He was also noted for his decency and sense of fair play. Under his guidance, the Irish Constabulary (Ireland) Act 1836 was introduced and paved the way forward for a positive restructuring of the force. This new act amalgamated the four provincial forces leaving them the responsibility for the policing of the whole country except the capital, which had its own Dublin Metropolitan Police. The 1822 and 1836 Acts established what become known as the Irish Constabulary.

This new body of men with their high standards of discipline were regarded as being very efficient and quite professional in their duties and policed Ireland as the Irish Constabulary up to 1867. In that year, in recognition of its loyalty and for its role in suppressing the Fenian Rising which occurred earlier that year, Queen Victoria honoured the Irish Constabulary with the title "Royal Irish Constabulary". Thus the RIC was born and served as the Irish police force from 1867 until it was disbanded in 1922 and replaced by a force known as the Civic Guard, but within a year renamed An Garda Síochána.

The Dublin Metropolitan Police (DMP) continued to serve independently until it was amalgamated with An Garda Síochána in 1925.

Policeman, Dundalk, 1834 Tempest's Annual, 1940.

This curious drawing is in the possession of Mr. T. G. F. Patterson, Curator, County Museum, Armagh, who has kindly sent us a photograph of it and given us the following details.

The identity of the artist, "H. B." is not known, but the sketch was made at the assizes here in that year. The churn-like hat is an exaggerated form of the flat-topped shako worn by some mounted troops in most European armies. The stick-like object must be a carbine and the truncheon handle appears behind his elbow.

The earliest illustration we have of a policeman in Dundalk is from Tempest's Annual, 1940, showing the drawing of a policeman with the caption "Policeman, Dundalk, 1st March 1834", a depiction of a member of a force which had such a powerful role in Irish life throughout the 19th century. In quiet times the RIC were tolerated as enforcers of law and order and were generally helpful to the community when possible, especially when form filling or other issues involving literacy arose, but when tense political and agrarian situations occurred they were regarded as the strong right arm of British justice in Ireland. One such incident took place on Saturday 11th June 1881 when a famous eviction took place at Kilcroney, Knockbridge, approximately 7 miles outside Dundalk. At the time this was one of the major events in the north-east. According to historian Pat O'Neill in his *History of Knockbridge*, "A few days before the eviction the police were making enquiries as to the number of cars which might be forthcoming to convey from one hundred and twenty to one hundred and fifty constabulary to Kilcroney. But the poor car owners and car drivers had just been visited with a general and very curious

Site of Crawley Eviction.

epidemic. The Land League must be in possession of occult and magic powers for all at once every horse became ill or lame and where the horse escaped the cars had been attacked, wheels had mysteriously given way, tyres had fallen off and spokes had been consumed by spontaneous combustion. How then could the poor car men drive the police to Kilcroney? This is why the authorities decided on using a special train to Castlebellingham". This eviction led to the presence of two hundred RIC men plus two troops of the 19th Hussars from Dundalk Military Barracks whose duty it was to keep the peace and maintain law and order. Earlier that day the RIC men had arrived by train at Castlebellingham and marched the four miles to their destination. This was the only mode of travel made available to the authorities as all the local jarveys plus all other transport personnel had refused to transport the policeman to the eviction. Thousands of people turned up to support the Crawley family who were being evicted. A standoff that could have had serious repercussions with two hundred policemen involved was avoided because cool heads prevailed. With the strong influence of local clergy, an agreement was reached which allowed the eviction to proceed while the family was otherwise looked after. The eviction of Lawrence Crawley by Lord Louth was to be a turning point in Land Reform. Evictions like this were one of the most detestable duties that the RIC had to perform as most of them came from small farming holdings themselves.

Queen Victoria's Ceremonial Delegation from Dundalk district at Kingstown (now Dun Laoghaire, Co. Dublin), 1900.

Front Row Second from Right: Constable Daniel Holland based at Bridge Street.

(Photo: Courtesy Holland Family)

Moving from the 19th into the 20th century, policing in Dundalk and generally throughout Ireland appeared to be peaceful. From 1894 to 1903 the RIC District Inspector in charge of policing the Dundalk area was Thomas St George McCarthy, a man of great sporting distinction who in his younger days had represented Ireland on the rugby pitch and also became a co-founder of the Gaelic Athletic Association (GAA). Upon reaching Dundalk he had achieved the rank of District Inspector 2nd Class and two years later had achieved 1st Class status which is the equivalent to Garda Superintendent. His life story from both a national and local point of view is very interesting.

According to Marcus dé Búrca in his article *"The Curious Career of Sub-Inspector Thomas St George McCarthy"* from the Tipperary Historical Journal 1988, Thomas St George McCarthy was born on 11th June 1862 in Bansha, Co Tipperary, the son of a County RIC Inspector and Resident Magistrate. He was educated at Tipperary Grammar School where his rugby career began. He moved to Dublin in 1879 and got to know Michael Cusack, who was running a cramming school at the time. This school prepared young men for entry examinations to Trinity College, medical and law schools, plus army, navy and police cadetships. In Dublin McCarthy's rugby career blossomed, and in January 1882 he eventually got his place on the Irish International Rugby Team playing against Wales. Apart from his sporting success, while still under Michael Cusack's tutelage he got first place in an RIC cadetship examination and went on to join the RIC in 1882.

After training he was promoted to 3rd Class District Inspector and was allocated to Templemore, Co Tipperary. Possibly due to his friendship with Michael Cusack, eighteen months later he was present at the inaugural meeting of the Gaelic Athletic Association (GAA) in Hayes' Hotel, Thurles on November 1st 1884, and on that date his name was recorded as one of the founder members of the association. There was never any doubt regarding his love of sport or his sporting abilities, but after the initial meeting he did not come to the fore in GAA circles. This is possibly due to the strong nationalistic bias of the association at its foundation. In 1885 Michael Cusack declared that no athletes would be allowed to compete at GAA meetings if they competed elsewhere under different rules, and from 1888 onwards all serving members of the RIC and British Army were prohibited from playing GAA games.

In November 1887 McCarthy married Mary Lucy Lynch from the North Circular Road, Dublin. The marriage produced two children, a son and a daughter who in later life emigrated to Canada and Australia respectively. After serving in Derrygonnelly, Co Fermanagh and Limavady, Co Derry he was transferred to Dundalk on 1st December 1894 where he was to serve as District Inspector for the next nine years. His history file shows that while in Dundalk he received a severe reprimand for disobedience to orders, together with a warning about his future should he *"again refuse to carry out his duties loyally or give cause for complaint to the Inspector General"*. While in Dundalk he played for the local cricket team. Whatever happened in Dundalk, he appears to have fallen out of favour with his superiors as his following transfers were to stations of lesser importance. Eventually he retired on 23rd January 1912. His history file also states that he was placed on pension because he had become unfit for further duty on account of his general conduct and demeanour and the injuries he had received while on duty in 1894 in Dundalk.

After retirement he lived in Ranelagh, Dublin and seldom missed an All-Ireland hurling final in Croke Park or an International rugby game at Landsdowne Road. His days ended in a nursing home in Blackrock, and after his death on March 12th 1943 he was buried in nearby Deansgrange Cemetery in an unmarked grave. Overgrown for years, the grave was eventually discovered by RIC historian Jim Herlihy who put the wheels of recognition in motion. Later, as part of the "re-dedication of founders' graves" programme to mark the 125th anniversary of the founding of the GAA, the GAA authorities erected a commemorative gravestone at Deansgrange which was unveiled on 18th November 2009.

RIC Anne Street Barracks, circa 1906. (Photo: Courtesy Victor Whitmarsh)

*RIC Bridge Street Barracks, circa 1900
Back Row 5th Member from left: Daniel Holland.
(Photo: Courtesy Holland Family)*

By the early part of the 20th century three police barracks had been established in Dundalk. County and District HQ was based in Anne Street (now occupied by an apartment building named "St Anne's Court"). Number 2 Barracks was based at Clanbrassil Street (formerly Cumiskey's shop, now vacant) and later moved to Bridge Street (now Quinn's Funeral Undertakers). Number 3 Barracks was at the junction of Quay Street with Peter Street. The outlying barracks in Dundalk District were Blackrock, Ballymacscanlan, Greenore, Omeath, Carlingford, Castlebellingham and Louth Village. Times were relatively peaceful and continued so up to the Easter Rising.

RIC Quay Street Barracks.
Last RIC Station Party to serve at Quay Street RIC Station 1922, prior to disbandment.
Left to Right: Sergeant Taylor, ..., ..., Constable James Morrissey.
(Photo: Courtesy Morrissey Family)

The Easter Rising in 1916 had its consequences in Dundalk as in many other provincial towns. This is well documented with up to ninety armed Volunteers from the locality gathering at the Boyle O'Reilly premises in Clanbrassil Street and marching towards Dublin on Easter Sunday 23rd April 1916, to assist in the Rising. They were accompanied by a Sergeant Michael Wymes (whose son, also named Michael, later became Garda Commissioner) and a Sergeant Connolly, whose duty it was to monitor the Volunteers' movements. Unfortunately the following day an incident took place in Castlebellingham in which a young RIC constable named Charles McGee was shot dead.

Charles McGee was a young RIC constable based at Gilbertstown Barracks south of Dundalk. Born in 1892 and from Innisboffin, between the coast of Co Donegal and Tory Island, he was at first a fisherman. On 1st November 1912 he was appointed to the force having received his registration number 66908, and in May 1913 he was posted to serve in County Louth. By all accounts he was a popular young policeman in the area.

Constable Charles McGee.
(Photo: Courtesy Madge O'Boyle)

On that fateful day, Easter Monday 24th April 1916, he was based at Gilbertstown Barracks. Late in the evening he left his barracks in Gilbertstown and cycled with dispatches towards Castlebellingham. On his journey he was warned by local people to stay clear of Castlebellingham as it was known there was danger there. In spite of this warning he continued on his journey and upon arrival in Castlebellingham he was taken prisoner by the group of Volunteers who had earlier marched from Dundalk to join the Rising in Dublin. At Collon they were told the Rising had been cancelled, and they marched back towards Dundalk. At Lurgangreen, just south of Dundalk they were instructed by a messenger to return to Dublin as the Rising was indeed in progress in the city. On this return journey to Dublin they were stopped by Constable Donovan and Acting Sergeant Kiernan in Castlebellingham. The Volunteers, having taken charge of this situation, placed all the RIC men under arrest including Constable McGee upon his arrival. A passing car occupied by 2nd Lieutenant Robert Dunville of the Grenadier Guards and his driver were likewise halted and the two men were also taken captive. All the captives were placed together, with Lieutenant Dunville ending up beside Constable McGee. They were surrounded by approximately fifty men armed with rifles, shotguns, revolvers and some homemade weaponry. Suddenly one or possibly more of the rebels opened fire, wounding Lieutenant Dunville and killing Constable McGee, who became the first casualty of the Easter Rising in Co Louth. He was later buried in Gortahork, Co Donegal.

Three years after the Easter Rising came the War of Independence. On 21st January 1919 two RIC men, Constable James McDonnell and Constable Patrick O'Connell were ambushed and shot dead while escorting explosives to Soloheadbeg Quarry in Co Tipperary. These are accepted as the first killings in the War of Independence. This date also coincided with the establishment of Dáil Eireann.

In April 1919, as a result of a proposal by Eamon de Valera, a resolution was passed in Dáil Eireann approving the boycotting of the RIC. Having classified them as being "England's janissaries and the eyes and ears of the British Government", he proposed that they be ostracised publicly, socially and in any other way possible. This motion having been passed was to prove the beginning of the end of the force we now consider to be the "Old RIC". Over the next two years peace disappeared and was replaced with shootings, killings and attacks on police barracks during what became known as the War of Independence.

By the early 1920s, as a result of this ostracism, the strength of the RIC force became greatly depleted with many early resignations and retirements, leaving the force with as many as one thousand five hundred vacancies in the ranks of the regular RIC. This led the British Government to decide that the force needed to be strengthened, resulting in the recruitment of a force of special reserves from Great Britain, of which ninety-five percent who applied and were accepted were former British Army soldiers who were not long out of the trenches after World War One, and had experience only of soldiering rather than policing. They were later to become known as the Black and Tans due to their khaki tunics and navy trousers which resembled the colour of a pack of hounds in County Limerick, also known as the Black and Tans. Their police training lasted no more than three to four weeks, and having been sworn in as temporary constables, each of them was allocated an RIC number. The behaviour and attitude of the Black and Tans was hard enough for the Irish people to endure but what was yet to come was a lot worse - the dreaded Auxiliaries. The Auxiliary Division, like the Black and Tans, was hastily recruited in Great Britain and was meant to further strengthen the numbers of the RIC. Most of this new body were ex-officers of the British Army and were considered upper class and arrogant, believing themselves superior to both the Old RIC and their fellow Black and Tan comrades. After a short initial training (mostly in firearms) they also received an RIC number. These men were to change the character of the RIC. As history would later show they created murder and mayhem wherever they went either on duty or off duty. They turned out to be such a law unto themselves that even the established Old RIC policemen could not handle them. Approximately 8,800 Black and Tans and Auxiliaries were sent to Ireland to prop up the RIC with each county including Louth getting its quota. Approximately twenty to twenty five were stationed in the Dundalk area.

With this new era of confrontations between the police and the IRA, casualties were soon to follow. One such incident involved Constable Brennan, a native of Tubbercurry, Co. Sligo, who was to be the first casualty of the Crown Forces in Co Louth during the War of Independence. On Sunday afternoon 22nd August 1920 Sergeant Owen Clarke along with Constables Thomas Brennan, Joe Isdell and Ralph Witherden (all based at Quay Street Barracks) were on patrol in Jocelyn Street, Dundalk, going towards the town centre. As they passed the Catholic Young Men's Society building an incident occurred in which seven armed civilians ran out from Distillery Lane and started shooting at the policemen. As a result of the incident Constable Brennan was shot dead and Constables Isdell and Witherden were seriously injured. The following is an account of the incident given by Sergeant Clarke:

"The whole affair occurred at the corner of Distillery Lane. Constables Brennan, Witherden, Isdell and myself were coming up the town when a number of men rushed out from the corner. They made a half circle around us. Some of them shouted "Hands up!" and at the same time they all fired right into us. My comrades fell and a bullet passed through my belt and into portion of my tunic. Immediately they fired the fellows dashed away towards the football field and other places. I returned fire but they were some distance off".

On Monday evening 23rd August 1920 Constable Brennan's remains were removed from the Louth Infirmary to St Patrick's Cathedral and the following day after requiem mass his coffin was taken to the railway station for conveyance to Tubbercurry where he was laid to rest.

Further casualties were to follow, and perhaps one of the biggest RIC funerals to take place in Dundalk was that of Sergeant Timothy Holland who was ambushed and shot in Cullyhanna Co Armagh on a Feis Day on 6th June 1920. He succumbed to his wounds on 9th June 1920 at the Louth Infirmary. The Democrat and People's Journal at the time reported: *"On Thursday night the remains of Sergeant Holland, who was shot at Cullyhanna, Co Armagh on Saturday night were removed from the Louth Infirmary to the Dominican Church, Dundalk where the rosary was recited and the Dead March played. The remains were carried by his comrades and rested before the altar through the night. On Friday morning a most impressive funeral was accorded the remains which were being removed from the Church to the station for interment in Belfast. Full military honours were accorded the deceased. The coffin was draped in the Union Jack and Sergeant Holland's cap, belt and bayonet rested on a gun carriage drawn by six magnificent black chargers and driven by six sergeants from the Royal Field Artillery (RFA). A firing party of twelve men from the RFA with arms reversed, headed the cortege".* Sergeant Holland was later interred at Milltown Cemetery, Belfast with full military honours.

A further incident of an RIC policeman being fatally injured in the Dundalk area occurred on 17th June 1921 when Constable William Campbell, who was based at Bridge Street, Dundalk, did not return to his barracks for roll call at 11pm. Following a search his body was found at Dowdallshill on the Newry Road. Constable Campbell had been shot three times. He was buried on 22nd June 1921 in Dowdallshill Cemetery following a full ceremonial funeral of military and police. However, the aftermath of Constable Campbell's killing leaves a lot of questions unanswered. Within two hours of the killing of Constable Campbell two brothers, John and Patrick Watters, were taken from their home at the Windmill Bar, Seatown and shot dead. While not proven, it is highly suspected that the Auxiliaries were responsible for these murders as a reprisal.

Throughout Ireland approximately four hundred and twenty five RIC men were killed and seven hundred and twenty five were wounded in the period January 1919 to July 1921. Disbandment of the RIC commenced in 1922 and was more or less complete by September of that year. In

Dundalk and generally in the north-east the Old RIC was still held with respect by their communities while everybody was delighted to see the back of the Black and Tans and the Auxiliaries. Certainly, there was no animosity shown to the local members of the Old RIC who, after disbandment, settled locally in Dundalk and continued to raise their families.

Armed RIC Patrol at Roche Cross, Hackballscross, Dundalk, circa 1918.
(Photo: Courtesy Jimmy Bellew)

Constable James Morrissey, Quay Street, with his wife and family prior to disbandment.
(Photo: Courtesy Morrissey Family)

Perhaps the best description of the RIC exit from Dundalk was given by the Dundalk Democrat and People's Journal of 1st April 1922. The article seems to capture the true essence of what took place on 29th March 1922, when the RIC left the town.

"We had one result of the truce made apparent in Dundalk on Wednesday evening when the RIC in Dundalk evacuated their barracks in Bridge Street and Anne Street and companies of the IRA entered into possession.

For weeks there have been rumours of the evacuation; days were appointed for the task and then changed. But it came to a head on Wednesday and, truth to tell, Dundalk took it very quietly. We had no general holiday same as they had in other towns; we had very few flags flying and little cheering. It was not made the occasion of a demonstration - it was purely a business proposition, with one body of men making room for another.

There must have been about 150 people outside Bridge Street at 2 o clock, and of that number more than 100 were women and girls. A big Crossley was drawn up outside the door, and now and then a policeman emerged from the door and threw part of his belongings into the tender. Sometimes the youngsters in the crowd cheered at this move; more often they didn't. It was tiresome, this waiting. One lady did her best to dance a jig outside and she amused the crowd somewhat. The first announcement of the new order of things was when Mr John McGuill drove down in a motor. With him was Captain Donnelly, the liaison officer for the county. Captain Donnelly was taken into the Barracks by District Inspector Gallagher and remained there for perhaps half an hour. It was surmised that he was going through the formalities of getting possession. The crowd increased and awaited developments. The policeman in charge of the Crossley whiled away the time starting and stopping the engine and the little boys climbed on the car and enjoyed themselves. An athletic girl more curious than the rest managed to get on to the barrack windowsill and endeavoured to get a peep at those inside. She was hardly rewarded for her pains because the windows were coated with dust that had collected for the couple of years during which the front door was never opened except with caution and the place was piled high with sandbags. One noticed that the constabulary sign which used to adorn the front of the building had been removed and also the place could do with a coat of paint.

At length the door opened and out there came the station force – about 15 men all told. Each one of them carrying his rifle jumped into the waiting Crossley from which the boys had been evicted and drove off. That was the last RIC occupation of Bridge Street Barracks. There was a cheer raised and the police saluted in return. Then Captain Donnelly emerged and motored to Anne Street where later in the day a company of armed IRA men, marching well and carrying bandoliers, took possession of the barracks. On their entry a Sinn Féin flag was hoisted from a top window.

At Anne Street Barracks it was much the same. The police had been going up and down the street in cars taking their belongings with them. A fairly good crowd had collected and this narrow thoroughfare became blocked. Children were fairly numerous, and these commenced to throw old boots – of which there was a large and varied assortment strewn around – into a waiting car. One of these failed to reach the seat of the car and went instead through the windscreen. The car was just moving at the time so it was stopped and reversed. As this operation was in progress a sergeant happened to come along. He was knocked down by the car. The good cheer, which he got from the crowd, put him in good humour and he rose smiling. Then somebody "booed" as the car went away and one of the occupants is alleged to have drawn a revolver. Maybe he did; at all events he went no further with it.

Somewhere about 4 o clock a company of IRA marched through Park Street and entered into possession. They were heartily cheered and like their comrades in Bridge Street placed a large Republican Flag from one of the windows. That entire evening people congregated around the place – a curious crowd, waiting patiently for something to turn up. Inside however, the men were busy getting the place in order and there was nothing to report."

1922 brought to an end a turbulent era in the policing of Ireland. In Donal O'Sullivan's book *The Irish Constabularies 1822-1922* he remarked that during that era *"policing in Ireland stood at the perilous intersection of politics, religion and the relationship between Britain and Ireland"*. This would appear to be a fair and reflective summing up of that policing period.

Chapter 3
- 1922 to 1970 -

In 1922 the new Irish police force was initially referred to as the Civic Guard and its first commissioner was Michael Staines. His mission statement at the time was that this new force would succeed not by force of arms or numbers but on their moral authority as servants of the people. Michael Staines, while very proud to be the first Commissioner of this new force, was unfortunate to become embroiled in what became known as the Kildare Mutiny. This situation arose when the trainee guards in the Curragh refused to accept the authority of the ex-RIC men whom Michael Collins had put in charge of their training because of their loyalty to him. On 15th May 1922 Staines had to flee the training camp in Kildare when his leadership of the force became greatly undermined. Incidents like this led the Government to reassess the situation, resulting in Kevin O'Higgins taking over as Minister for Home Affairs and ordering an enquiry into the mutiny. Eventually the situation was resolved and on 11th September 1922 General Owen O'Duffy (a County Monaghan man) was appointed as the second Commissioner of this new force. This appointment is believed to have been made solely on the merit of his capabilities and proven organisational abilities.

It did not take Commissioner O'Duffy long to set out his stall, and knowing who the troublemakers were within the force he quickly weeded them out. Known as a strict disciplinarian, he demanded a high standard from his men, his attitude being – if you don't like these standards, get out. According to the Garda Review of 1929, part of his address in November 1922 to the recruits heading to their various stations throughout the country went as follows: *"The Civic Guard is to be strictly non–political. It is a police force for all the people and not for any section of the people. It is not their business how the people think politically, everyone is entitled to their opinion – these as they may be. They are prohibited from taking part in politics, from associating with one side more than another. They will serve whatever Government the people of Ireland put into office and as far as they can they will protect the lives and property of all the people. The Civic Guard is to be an unarmed force. I take certain responsibility for this step and I do not regret it. An unarmed force depends entirely for its success on the moral support of the people"*. As for those members heading for the troublesome regions, his advice was, *"Don't open your doors, let them be smashed in; don't surrender your property or that entrusted to your charge; defend it with your lives. Far better the grave than dishonour. Don't be alarmed by the sound of a shot. You heard it before and you were not subdued because you had right on your side and the gunman had only might. I know the stuff you are made of and I know you would not allow me, if I wanted to, to retain in the Civic Guard a weakling who would take off his uniform and hand it over to any coward who had never fought before"*. So with this verbal motivation behind them the new Civic Guard went out to police a New Ireland.

This new unarmed police force was generally accepted by the people. However, in some areas, especially where there was a strong anti-treaty sentiment, stations were attacked and burned, along with other acts of vandalism. In the first twelve months of the Civic Guards' existence it is estimated that over two hundred stations were attacked and burned. Hundreds of members were assaulted and beaten up and one member, Garda Harry Phelan, was murdered in Mullinahone, Co. Tipperary. By comparison, other members were warmly greeted upon arrival at their destination, with local people helping them to get settled in.

Dundalk was to get its share of this new police force with both Anne Street and Bridge Street being occupied by the Civic Guards in early November 1922. The following is a description of their arrival by the local Democrat and People's Journal on Saturday 4th November 1922:

"The long expected Civic Guards arrived on Tuesday. The first thing they did was to remove the elaborate sand bag barricades and entrenchments from the front of Anne Street Barrack which they had taken over from the military and the place no longer looks like a beleaguered outpost in Waziristan. One result of this will probably be that people in Anne Street and Park Street will be allowed to sleep in peace at night. For months past Anne Street barrack has been the pretty safe and obvious target of the gentle sniper, couched in some clump in the Demesne; and residents around have come to apprehend that there are more sedative things than a sniper's bullet hopping of the roof at regular intervals between nightfall and 4 a.m. The Civic Guard being an unarmed force there will be no excuse for sniping their quarters. But if anyone thinks that because they are unarmed they can be safely disregarded he is mistaken. They are big hefty fellows of very much the type of the old RIC men, recruited no doubt from the same farming population for the most part. They look as if they could use their fists, not to speak of their truncheons, very effectively.

Now that the Civic Guards are here we shall probably have to toe the line of legality in a whole lot of small matters as to which we have for some months past lived in comfortable disregard for the law. The lad who feels he wants a small drink on Sunday will no longer be able to saunter up to the agreeable publican's door and claim admission with a loud and careless knock. The days have come again when he will have to take the word from the "sentry" at the street corner and slip round by the back way when the coast is clear. The lad who rides a bicycle by night will once more have to think up excuses for not having his lamp lighted. The lads who have been signalising the dawn of freedom by smashing street lamps and windows will have to find recreation less risky than organised stone throwing. Petty larcenists and "hold-ups" will have maybe to look for work. May we mention as worthy of attention in the spare time of the Civic Guards, the herds of roving goats that work such havoc in front gardens and park plantations. There is quite a lot of work for the boys in blue – very nice blue it is. We wish them the height of luck and bespeak for them the sympathy and co-operation of every law abiding citizen."

Bridge Street Station Party, circa 1927.
Seated Left to Right: John Murray, Sgt. James Guilfoyle, Edward Rahilly (with Bubbles), Patrick Denver, Sgt. Edward Flood, Sgt. Malachy Kealy.
Back Row: Thomas Duncan, Stn. Sgt Richard Wheelan, Charles Lynch, James Beatty, ... , W. Carroll, James Delaney, Sgt. James Dermody, Sgt. Patrick Campbell, Supt. Herbert Lea.
(Photo: Courtesy Iris an Gharda)

Anne Street Station Party, circa 1925-1926.
Back Row: J. Kissane, A. Hayes, …, W. Stephens, J. Nyhan.
Middle Row: T. McGuinness, J. Ryan, J. Shortall, F. Mohan, J. Butler, J. Murphy, M. Crummy, P. Reid.
Seated: J. Lennon, Sgt. M Morgan, Supt. J. Feore, Insp. T. Kelly, Sgt. P Bohan, J. Concagh, Mascot "Kerry".
(Photo: Courtesy Iris an Gharda)

During the early 1920s the new Civic Guards seemed to have settled well into Anne Street and Bridge Street. On 31st July 1923 a Government amendment bill was passed renaming the force "An Garda Síochána". By this stage the new Government had chosen to adapt the old successful policing system of the RIC and under the Garda Síochána Act 1924 the words "Garda Síochána" were substituted for any previous legal reference to the "RIC". As a result a disciplined policing system was to continue with the consent of the people.

Commissioner O'Duffy's main influence on the force was to make sure that the new Gardaí got out there and mixed with the people. His approach was: you are from the people, you belong to the people, and you mix with them, play sport with them but above all gain their respect. Perhaps he was ahead of his time with the concept of community policing. One of his main aims was to get most of these young Gardaí actively involved in sports and he encouraged them to get involved with local teams. One initiative to further this aim was to set up Garda Sports Days and this was successfully achieved in Dundalk. From perusal of a programme of the 1932 Garda Sports event in my possession, it is evident that not weeks but months of preparation had gone into the running of this event with major involvement from the local community. All the prizes were sponsored; P.J.Carroll & Co, Ltd, cigarette manufactures, supplied the sound system, and the local Superintendent, T.S. Mc Donagh, officiated as the chief field steward on the day. The thank you credit on the programme simply read *"The Committee wish to thank all those who assisted the Guards in the organisation of the sports and the many friends who presented prizes or those whose subscription enabled such excellent prizes to be given. They also thank the general public for the support accorded the fixture."* The Garda Sports Day became one of the main calendar events of the year in Dundalk.

Crime Scene, Dundalk district, circa 1926.
(Photo: Courtesy Jimmy Bellew)

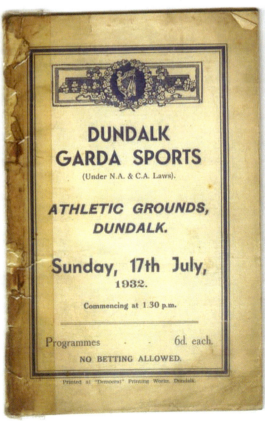

Booklet - Dundalk Garda Sports, 17th July 1932.

Although Dundalk and Co Louth received plenty of new Gardaí, Co Louth's contribution to the force was quite minimal. According to Liam McNiffe *(A History of An Garda Síochána)*, of the 32 counties' contribution from 1922 to 1932, Co Louth lay third from the bottom with 58 recruits in comparison to Cork - 658, Kerry - 576, and Mayo - 576. The two counties that lay below Louth were Antrim - 56, and Down - 50. This begs the question - what was the reason for these low figures from Co. Louth? Perhaps better employment prospects were available in Louth as at the time Dundalk had a busy port and a number of breweries plus other industries, or simply there was no interest in joining the new Garda Force. However, with thanks to the Henry family formerly of Anne Street, some interesting documentation came to light with regard to the original application of Edward Henry, Anne Street, Dundalk, to join the Gardaí. In it he states that he was employed as a boilermaker in the local GNR works but due to the depression in the trade he

I hereby testify to the good character of Edward Henry, Ann St. Dundalk. He belongs to a respectable family in this parish, and is strictly honest and sober. I can confidently recommend him as a suitable candidate for the Civic Guards.

*Charles Hurson Adm.
St Patrick's
11th August 1925. Dundalk*

A character reference for Edward Henry from the Rev. Charles Hurson, Adm. St Patrick's Dundalk.

was dismissed and was now offering himself as a candidate for the Gardaí. The application was accompanied by a character reference from the Rev Charles Hurson, Administrator of Saint Patrick's, Dundalk and dated 11th August 1925. Edward Henry was successful with his application and served most of his career in the Dublin Metropolitan Area.

While researching other personnel from the locality who joined the Gardaí in its infancy I came across a very interesting story relating to a young man from Dromiskin (four miles south of Dundalk) who, after being injured in the trenches in World War One, went on to join the Dublin Metropolitan Police. He later became a Garda and upon retirement from the Gardaí opened up a sub post office in Quay Street, Dundalk.

Thomas Kinahan was born in Dromiskin in 1893. His father was a farmer who owned a small holding of 14 acres on which he reared a family of ten. On 23rd November 1914, possibly due to a lack of employment or seeking a chance to see the world, Thomas, along with his younger brother James, joined the army, enlisting in Dundalk. James, only seventeen at the time and lying about his age, appeared to have no problem joining. Both enlisted in the Irish Guards regiment and after training were posted to France. Both of them were badly wounded in the trenches but were some of the lucky ones who lived to tell the tale. Thomas survived gunshot wounds to the face and shoulder, which were to trouble him again in later life, while James suffered serious arm injuries. Thomas's discharge papers show that he served the full period of the war and the medals received were the 1914-15 Star Medal, the British War Medal and the Victory Medal. These medals are still in the possession of the family. On 25th April 1919, after the war had ended, Thomas joined the Dublin Metropolitan Police (DMP) and was later appointed as a detective to the infamous "G" squad, which was known to be the bane of Michael Collins's life. His official registered number was 11481, and after the birth of the Free State Thomas continued to serve in the Dublin Metropolitan Area. When the amalgamation of the DMP and the Garda Síochána took place on 3rd April 1925 he automatically became a Detective Garda. Eventually, after a

Thomas and James Kinahan.
(Photo: Courtesy Harriet Andrews)

*Detective Garda Thomas Kinahan.
(Photo: Courtesy Harriet Andrews)*

*Thomas Kinahan's War Medals.
(Photo: Courtesy Harriet Andrews)*

distinguished career of thirty-one years' service, Thomas retired from An Garda Síochána on 6th April 1950 on full pension. However, Thomas's career was not to end there. He eventually made his way back to Dundalk where he opened up a sub post office in Quay Street and remained there until his second retirement in 1964. By this stage ill health was taking its toll as a result of the injuries he had received in the trenches and in 1965, after being declared medically unfit, he applied for and received his war pension. On a further note, Thomas's brother James, mentioned earlier, emigrated to England after the war and set up home there. His son went on to join the British Army, rising to the rank of Brigadier General.

I thank Thomas's grand-daughter, Harriet Andrews, for giving me this very interesting story which is accompanied by documentary proof and photographs.

While the new Gardaí became established in the locality as the new police force, their lack of experience in the investigation of serious crime was shown at different times. Perhaps this is best exemplified in the Mary Callan murder of 1927 at Faughart. Mary Callan, the priest's housekeeper, went missing on 16th May 1927. Three days later on 19th May, Fr McKeown notified Gardaí of her disappearance. As nothing appeared to be happening he called two days later to speak to the Sergeant in Charge, but still no investigation appeared to follow. Mary Callan's brother then called to the station and as a result two Gardaí came to the priest's house and questioned three people - the priest, a close friend of Mary Callan's, and a possible suspect. They said a Superintendent would call the next day, but this never occurred and all police activity seemed to wane. On 7th April 1928 the chief suspect left the area intent on travelling to Canada, but before he left Ireland he was arrested for stealing and returned to Dundalk. Eventually a Superintendent Hunt, an experienced crime investigator, arrived on the scene from Garda Headquarters, and using his experience set up a proper investigation. His investigation led to the local quarry being pumped out for four days and nights until eventually a female torso was found. The investigation continued until the chief suspect, Gerard Toal, was arrested. He was later tried and found guilty of the murder of Mary Callan and his execution took place on 29th August 1928.

The Mary Callan Murder Scene. Gardaí under Supt. Feore pump Capt. Bell's Quarry in search of Mary Callan's body. (Photo: Courtesy Jimmy Bellew)

In those early days a Garda was posted during daylight hours at the customs post at the border with Northern Ireland and also at the railway station. Overleaf is a rare photograph of Gardaí and RUC in uniform together. I am told this was part of a combined investigation, the details of which have been lost in time

Garda Patrick Campbell (No. 480) on duty at Dundalk Customs Station at Newry Road Bridge, circa 1926. (Photo: Courtesy Garda Archives)

Cross Border Crime Investigation, circa 1926. Local Gardaí with RUC Officers, Extreme Right: Garda Insp. T Kelly. (Photo: Courtesy Jimmy Bellew)

After the election on 16th February 1932 Eamon De Valera and the Fianna Fáil party came to power. In February the following year De Valera dismissed Eoin O'Duffy as leader of the force and replaced him with Chief Superintendent Eamonn Broy, picking him over the heads of four Deputy Commissioners and one Assistant Commissioner. De Valera was now shaping the force his way and putting his own men in key positions. During the early 1930s, politics was causing friction in Garda HQ, while Gardaí throughout the country were caught between the IRA, which opposed the 1922 Anglo-Irish treaty, and the Army Comrades Association (Blue Shirts), who had supported the Treaty. While serious disturbances occurred throughout the rest of the country, Dundalk and County Louth generally remained fairly stable and Gardaí policed the area without difficulty.

Linguaphone Lessons in Open Air at Dundalk, August 1931. (Photo: Courtesy Iris an Gharda)

During the years of the Second World War, known in Ireland as the Emergency, Dundalk Gardaí worked with the Local Defence Force (LDF) and although times were difficult they met the challenges which arose. Perhaps an example of their duties is best described by Kevin Gaynor in Victor Whitmarsh's *Dundalk in the Emergency*, in which Kevin states *"I was one of the first to join the Local Defence Force in Anne Street Barracks and if I am not mistaken the man who took me on was either Garda Mc Kiernan, or Garda Tom Clerkin who was known as the Railway Guard. We used to enjoy our guard duties in Anne Street Barracks. The barracks had an armoury that contained 500 rifles and the LDF had to detail men for guard duty there. It started at 8 pm and lasted 12 hours until 8 am the following morning. We went on duty for 2 hours and had 4 hours off and then back on again for 2 hours on and 4 hours off. We also did routine guard duty in Bridge Street Garda Barracks."*

In May 1940 the LDF (previously known as the Local Security Force - LSF), had two groupings, A and B. The A group was a paramilitary formation bearing arms, while the B group was a police auxiliary. The recruitment and organisation of these groups was the responsibility of the Gardaí, and locally Superintendent Mc Donagh, Inspector Crotty and Garda O Brien took charge with Garda O Brien being appointed as the Administrative Officer. Later in 1941 the A group was reclassified as the LDF coming under the control of the army with the Gardaí assisting in some of the administrative responsibilities. Their district command centre was situated in a wing of the old jail while their armoury was secured in Anne Street Garda Station. The B group was to remain on as an auxiliary police force and be of assistance to the Gardaí when requested. The training and quality of these new organisations were to be truly tested over the following years.

In December 1940 the first of four war planes to crash in the North Louth area during the Emergency landed just south of the border at Dungooley Cross. The plane was a Royal Air Force war plane and had gone off course due to bad weather conditions. In trying to take off again it crashed. A party of LDF were first on the scene and secured the area. The Gardaí later arrived and took the two crew members into custody and brought them to Bridge Street Garda Station. They were later handed over to the Army authorities. Both were unarmed.

In September 1941 a Canadian aircraft crashed at Aghameen near Jenkinstown, Dundalk, killing its crew of three. It was an unarmed aircraft that had travelled earlier in the night from Canada. Having fuel problems it had been given permission to land at Baldonnel Aerodrome, and after repairs the Department of External Affairs gave permission for the flight to continue on its journey to Aldergrove in Northern Ireland. Unfortunately, possibly because of heavy fog, it crashed at Aghameen with the loss of all its crew members. Their bodies were later taken to Dundalk military barracks. The Gardaí along with the other relevant authorities carried out their own investigations.

The third crash took place at Slieve Na Gloic Mountain, also in the Jenkinstown area, when a British Liberator bomber crashed into the side of the mountain with the loss of life of eighteen airmen. The flight had taken off from Egypt at 3 am on 5th March 1942 destined for the South of England. Apparently weather conditions were very bad leading to faults in the wireless equipment, and while flying up the Irish coast the Captain decided he would try and make it to an aerodrome in Northern Ireland. Unfortunately they never made it, crashing into the side of the mountain at 8 am the following morning. The crash site was in rough terrain and quite inaccessible which left it very difficult for the search and rescue operation that was to follow. Again, all the different authorities worked successfully together in the search and rescue of this terrible tragedy. The Garda investigation team was led by Superintendent McDonagh and Detective Sergeant McCabe. There were nineteen airmen on board the plane. Fourteen of them were found dead at the scene, four more later died from their injuries and there was one survivor, an Argentinian sergeant named Cyril Rowland Amos.

The final air crash of the Emergency occurred on 14th September 1944 at Dawestown,

Ravensdale, Dundalk, when an American Mustang fighter aircraft crashed. The pilot was found dead at the scene and was later identified by a gold bracelet he was wearing. The bracelet was inscribed with his name and number, and the donor as "Love Murph". The Gardaí, the army and the Red Cross were all involved in the follow up search and rescue operation.

In 1946 both Anne Street and Bridge Street Garda Stations closed down with all personnel moving to their new District Headquarters at the Crescent. This building was formerly the Governor's Residence of the old jail and to this day District HQ is still based there.

Garda Peter Coogan on duty at Blackrock Road, Dundalk, early 1950s. (Photo: Courtesy Duggan Family)

The post war years and the 1950s were to be one of the most peaceful periods in Ireland since the foundation of the state. However, throughout that era, hostilities broke out in the North every now and then, and as a result extra Gardaí were sent to the Border areas. One story from this quiet period came my way from Ex-Garda Sergeant Michael Mullany. Michael was the sergeant in charge of Omeath Garda Station from October 1967 until his retirement in June 1995 and can only be described as a legend and father figure to the many young Gardaí who served at his station during the troubles of the seventies and eighties. I am very grateful to Michael for this account recounted in his own unique way relating to the arrival of a Garda at Omeath Garda Station in 1956.

Local Gardaí Tom McGinn and Bill McGeogh on patrol at Main Street, Blackrock, circa 1950. (Photo: Courtesy Duggan Family)

Commissioner's Inspection in Dundalk Station Yard, early 1950s. (Photo: Courtesy Paul Kavanagh Collection)

*Dundalk Station Party, 1956.
Back Row: Tom Haverty, Sgt. Pat McCormack, John Hanlon, Tom Creehan, Nicholas Byrne, Frank McGrory, John Sexton, Jim Corry, Jim Conkey, ..., Rick Grogan.
Middle Row: Frank Delaney, Jim McNeilis, Charlie McElwaine, Peter Kavanagh, Pat O Brien, Joe Gaffney, Terry Reilly, George Comerford, Ned Kavanagh.
Front Row: Sgt. John Kennedy, D/Sgt. James McCabe, Sgt. Ned Sullivan, Supt. Thomas McDonagh, Insp. Michael Kealy, Sgt. Paddy McLoughlin (Later to become Garda Commissioner).
(Photo: Courtesy Paul Kavanagh Collection)*

One member who appeared to enjoy his stay in Omeath was Séamus O'Donnell. In a recent telephone call to the writer Séamus recalled with gusto an account of his first visit to Omeath. Along with a colleague, Hugh J. McGuire, he was transferred to Omeath from Navan in November 1956 shortly after an outbreak of hostilities in the North. He was driving his own car and accompanied by Hugh J. McGuire. As they drove along the coast road at North Commons they could see the bright lights of a town in the distance. Assuming that this was Omeath they were more than impressed. It was the nearest thing to Fairyland.

Buoyed up by the prospect of reaching a first class station, they drove merrily along with youthful abandon. As the well-lit town seemed to disappear from the radar the two were anxious and decided that all was not well. In pitch darkness there was no public lighting; or nobody about as far as they could see. A very tall Customs Officer stopped them at the Eire Customs Post. Hughie asked for directions to Omeath to which the Customs Officer replied, "Sure you're after coming from it". Not at all satisfied with the situation the officer decided to pry a little further and the boys felt obliged to declare their predicament.

Now satisfied that all was in order, the Officer told the driver to go back as far as the village and park at the terrace on the left: they could then cross the road to the Garda Station. The directions were one hundred percent accurate. As Séamus performed the three point turn, without the aid of power steering, the Customs Officer looked on. As they were about to move off he delivered his parting shot with a sense of humour. "In all my travels I have never come across two policemen who couldn't find their own Station". Before too long it transpired that the Custom Officer was none other than the well-known Richard Jacob. The two men reported to their station and commenced their day-to-day routine on Border duty.

As a Gaelic footballer Seamie was in the top grade, and he played for Cooley Kickhams. Soon he was selected to play for the County and in 1957 Louth won the Leinster Championship. Louth defeated Tyrone in the All-Ireland semi-final and went on to beat the much fancied Cork team in the final played on 22nd September at Croke Park before 72,000 spectators. Seamie had a great game and secured an All-Ireland medal, which he has treasured to this day.

Football aside, Seamie served in Omeath for three years before moving on transfer to Athboy. He pursued a successful career in the force, rising to the rank of Superintendent.

During these quiet years one incident stands out as it resulted in two local members receiving Silver Scott Medals for bravery. On 14th April 1962 a farmer residing in a rural area outside Dundalk suddenly became mentally unwell. Having placed his two dogs in a sack in the kitchen of his

Sgt. Michael Duggan with local Gardaí at Blackrock, early 1950s. (Photo: Courtesy Duggan Family)

Insp. Michael Kealy, Mr P. Woods (State Solicitor), Supt. Thomas McDonagh outside Dundalk Courthouse at the Circuit Court Sittings, circa 1950s. (Photo: Courtesy McDonagh Family)

Patrol Car at Dundalk, 1957.
Left to Right: Garda Tom Brophy, Garda Joe Gaffney. (Photo: Courtesy Paul Kavanagh Collection)

Members of Dundalk Station Party, 1960.
Left to Right: Sgt. McCormack, Tom Brophy, Tom Haverty, Frank Delaney, Dermot Winston, Frank McCague, Jim Kavanagh, Gerry Clifford, Pat O'Brien.
(Photo: Courtesy Paul Kavanagh Collection)

house, which he shared with his sister, he discharged two shots from a shotgun into the sack, killing the dogs. His sister fled from the house and notified the local doctor. Meanwhile a neighbour called to the house and found it locked up. He identified himself to the demented occupant, who in turn discharged a shotgun from inside the house. The local doctor, having failed to gain access, reported the matter to the Gardaí. Inspector Daniel Kennedy and another Garda arrived at the house around midnight. Attempts were made to get the man to surrender the shotgun and leave the house, but to no avail. While the two Gardaí looked through a rear window with the aid of torches the man discharged seven shots at them through the window. The man then escaped from the house and was later located by Gardaí, at whom he discharged two more shots before escaping. He was located at 6.30 am the next morning in the house of an elderly couple, standing guard at the half door with his shotgun. At 7.30 am Inspector Kennedy and Garda Jeremiah Clifford gained access to the house via a gable window. They managed to tackle the gunman and after a violent struggle they disarmed him. The shotgun was found to be loaded in both barrels.

Garda Jeremiah Clifford, Silver Scott Medal, 1962.

Inspector Daniel Kennedy, Silver Scott Medal, 1962.

For outstanding courage and devotion to duty the Silver Scott Medal was awarded to both Inspector Daniel Kennedy and Garda Jeremiah Clifford on 26th April 1963.

This was the first presentation of Scott Medals to members from Dundalk District. Over the following decades many more were to follow, some unfortunately under very tragic circumstances. The Scott Medal itself is the highest award for bravery that can be awarded to any member of An Garda Síochána, provided certain criteria are fulfilled. According to An Garda Síochána sources, its origins began in America in 1923 when Colonel Walter Scott, an Honorary Commissioner of the New York City police and a well-known philanthropist, presented An Garda Síochána, at the time the world's youngest police force, with a $1,000 gold bond. There is only one condition attached to the award of the Scott Medal. "No action, however heroic, will merit the award of the Scott Medal unless it takes the shape of an act of personal bravery, performed intelligently in the execution of duty at imminent risk to the life of the doer, and armed with full previous knowledge of the risk involved".

In 1967 a serious outbreak of foot-and-mouth disease occurred in Great Britain. Although the disease did not occur in Northern Ireland all our Border crossings had to be manned for what was classified as veterinary protection. Gardaí were deployed from all over the country to assist in this protection for the benefit of our own agriculture and economy. Dundalk Garda District had its own thirty six official Border crossings to man along with monitoring the areas in between. As there were very few privately cars owned then, the Gardaí were dropped off at their respective checkpoints with their flask and sandwiches and were eventually relieved after anything from four to twelve hours. It is acknowledged that local people living in the Border area looked after them very well and made sure they were well taken care of. Again, according to local people, accommodation was provided for the Gardaí in the former Blackrock Hotel now known as "The Brake".

The quarter century between the mid-1940s and 1970 was, on the whole, a quiet time for policing in Ireland. However, this proved to be the calm before the storm. As the 1970s opened this peace was shattered by the re-emergence of violent conflict in Northern Ireland. Policing in Ireland, and in Dundalk in particular, would be challenged and changed as never before.

Detective Garda Ned Kavanagh's Retirement, November 1964.
Back Row Left to Right: Tom Haverty, Joe Gaffney, RUC, RUC, Joe Barry, Dan Murphy, Seamus Flynn, Tony McDonagh, John Hickey, Ned O'Connor, Tom McEvaddy, Tony O Hanlon, John Shea, Donal Duffy.

Front Row: John Hanlon, Nicky Byrne, Michael McGowan, Leo Cosgrove, Frank Delaney, Jimmy McCabe, Jim Durkin, Johnny Byrne, …, Ned Kavanagh, Tom McDonagh, Martin Naughton, Michael Coleman, John Carville, Kevin Fleming, Frank McGrory, Mick Brady, Steve Faughan, Pat O Brien.

(Photo: Courtesy Paul Kavanagh Collection)

Commissioners Inspection Dundalk Station 23rd June 1966.

Commissioner's Inspection Dundalk Station, 23rd June 1966.
Back Row Left to Right: Eddie Murray, Edwin Hancock, Pat Slattery, Con Nolan, Tony Hanlon, Leo Cosgrove, Charley McCarron, George Flynn, Pat McAuliffe, Hugh McGinley, Brian McCabe, Harry Murtagh, John Harty, Tony McDonagh, Bill McCarthy, Donal Duffy, Vincent Reilly, Brendan Cunnane.

Middle Row: Jim O'Shea, Martin Naughton, Kevin Harrington, Joe Gaffney, Fintan Kenny, Terry Fanning, John O'Connell, Jim Soraghan, Jim Lane, Ned Smith.

Front Row: Joe O'Donovan, John Hickey, John Shea, Michael Connolly, Jim Durkin, Bill Grier, Joseph Downey, Denis Daly.

Seated: Insp. Joseph McGovern, Commissioner William Quinn, Supt. John Byrne.
(Photo: Courtesy Paul Kavanagh Collection)

Chapter 4
- 1970s -

The 1970s were to prove a very violent era throughout Ireland and Dundalk was to have its fair share of it. Armed robberies, especially at local post offices, were now the norm. Gone were the good old-fashioned days of the 1950s and 1960s when solving crime and keeping simple law and order were standard practice. New offences being brought before the courts related to abductions, shootings, possession of firearms with intent to endanger life, possession of explosives, hijackings, kidnappings and illegal membership of unlawful organisations.

Political and civil unrest was taking place in Northern Ireland and serious border incidents were beginning to occur. As a result more Gardaí were transferred from further south to border stations. Dundalk Garda District with its thirty six official border crossings had three border sub districts, Omeath, Dromad and Hackballscross to maintain plus the other two sub districts of Blackrock and Louth village.

Following the outbreak of this unrest and the spillover of the violence south of the border, the Irish Government sent troops to the border areas in support of the Gardaí. Some of these troops were sent to Aiken Military Barracks, Dundalk and on 1st September 1973 they became officially established as the 27th Infantry Battalion. Over the next thirty years they played a very important role in giving armed protection to uniformed Gardaí on checkpoint duty throughout the border area. Other joint duties lay in escorting large sums of money, industrial explosives and the escort of high security prisoners. From a Garda perspective I have no doubt in stating that if the uniformed Gardaí on checkpoint duty in the Border areas did not have the armed protection of the 27th Battalion, lives would have been lost.

Many incidents began to happen along the border, but perhaps one of the earliest incidents was later known as "The Battle of Courtbane". An incursion by the British Army occurred on 29th August 1971 when two Ferret scout cars based in Crossmaglen crossed the border and drove for a mile into the south. When the locals became aware of this incursion they surrounded the two scout cars as they tried to turn back, blocking their way with materials used to block border roads.

Shooting incident at Courtbane, Hackballscross, August 1971.

(Photo: courtesy Paul Kavanagh Collection)

The soldiers managed to leave their vehicles and cross the border, and two of them later returned and retrieved one of the vehicles. The other vehicle had been looted and set alight. An IRA unit became involved and exchanged gunfire with the British Army on the northern side. As a result of the gunfire a British Army soldier was shot dead and another seriously injured. Political controversy ensued following this incident with the British Government claiming the Gardaí were slow to respond, and Jack Lynch, the then Taoiseach, claiming that the constant incursion by the British Army into the south was causing distress to the local community. A Garda investigation into the incident concluded that all the gunfire had taken place north of the border.

Very soon afterwards another serious incident that took place locally, now mostly forgotten, was the infamous "Battle of Dungooley" as it later became known. On 27th January 1972 at around 8 am an IRA unit engaged the British Army in a serious exchange of gunfire at Dungooley which lies on the border between north Louth and south Armagh. Shortly after the exchange started Gardaí under the direction of Superintendent Richard Fahy arrived at the scene, and as they were unarmed, they remained at a discreet distance from the gunfire while the battle raged on for about two hours. An Irish Army unit arrived but by this stage the battle was easing off. As a group of young men left the scene their names were taken, and, being unarmed, they were allowed to go their way. Later in follow-up searches firearms and an antitank gun were found. The British army admitted to firing 2,550 rounds of ammunition into the South and they estimated that over 500 rounds were fired at them. Remarkably no one was shot or wounded in this incident. A short time later seven men were arrested and charged in connection with the battle. While these men were in custody events took place in Derry on 30th January 1972, which became known as Bloody Sunday, when thirteen unarmed civil rights demonstrators were shot dead by British Army paratroopers. This caused public opinion in Dundalk, and throughout Ireland, to turn sympathetic to the republican movement, and after a number of highly charged court appearances the charges were eventually dropped.

A further major incident which occurred in 1972 was the previously mentioned riot which took place on the evening of 21st September when Dundalk Garda Station was attacked by a riotous mob and the town itself suffered the aftermath with serious consequences. The result of this attack meant that extra personnel were immediately deployed to the area, some permanently and others on temporary transfer with the main purpose being to establish normality and security for the town and its residents.

Front of Dundalk Garda Station after riots, September 1972. Note the security box in front of station, manned 24 hours daily. (Photo: courtesy Paul Kavanagh Collection)

Over the following years local Gardaí in the normal course of their duty were to find themselves in open confrontation with gunmen. One of the earliest examples of this occurred on 14th December 1972 when Inspector Thomas Walsh and Detective Sergeant Myles Hawkshaw along with other Gardaí went to carry out a search for firearms at a farmer's residence and outhouses in the Dundalk area. Approaching the premises the detective sergeant saw a man look out the door of a shed which was about ten yards away to his right. Immediately the man disappeared into the shed, closing the door. Suddenly the door of the shed burst open and four men rushed out of it with the last man carrying a .303 rifle and wearing two bandoliers of ammunition. Three of the men ran towards an exit to their right and were pursued by the Gardaí who caught two of them. The detective sergeant moved in on the gunman who at this stage was only a few feet away. The gunman turned around and pointed the rifle at him. Detective Sergeant Hawkshaw shouted, "*Don't fire, don't fire!*" and at the same time he rushed the gunman, grabbed the rifle, and a struggle ensued. Inspector Walsh also rushed the gunman, tackling him from behind. Together they knocked the gunman to the ground and overpowered him while another member of the search party took possession of the rifle. On examination it was found that it was fully loaded and had one round up the breech. Three rifles and two bandoliers of ammunition were found during the search of the shed used by the four men

Inspector Tom Walsh, Bronze Scott Medal, 1972.

Detective Sergeant Myles Hawkshaw, Silver Scott Medal, 1972.

For bravery and devotion to duty Detective Sergeant Myles Hawkshaw was awarded the Silver Scott Medal and Inspector Thomas Walsh received the Bronze Scott Medal.

On 5th May 1973 as the result of a tragic accident, Garda John Lally was the first Garda to lose his life while on duty in the Dundalk area. On that date a major security operation was taking place in Dundalk and Gardaí from outside districts and divisions were transferred in to assist. Garda John Lally was based in Carrickmacross, Co Monaghan and was transferred to Dundalk for the day. His duty was to man a checkpoint on the Ardee/Dundalk road for the duration of the operation, but that evening he was accidentally knocked down by a passing vehicle and later died from his injuries. Originally from Belmullet, Co Mayo, Garda Lally was just short of one year's service in An Garda Síochána when this tragic event occurred.

Garda John Lally, accidentally killed on duty, 5th May 1973.

As we advanced into the 1970s armed robberies became very prevalent with many incidents taking place involving firearms. One such incident occurred on Sunday 10th August 1975 at Church Street, Dundalk. On that date Detective Garda Denis Daly went to Church Street to investigate an alleged shooting incident. A large crowd had gathered there and the detective Garda was told that a man who had been shot in the head was being cared for in a nearby house. A man walking away from the scene was identified to him as being the one who did the shooting and he was told that this man was armed. The Detective Garda, who was unarmed, followed the gunman into a crowded licensed premises, walked up behind him to arrest him, but as he touched him the gunman drew

Detective Garda Denis Daly, Silver Scott Medal, 1976.

a revolver from the waistband of his trousers and swung around sharply. Although obstructed by a civilian, the detective Garda disarmed the gunman and took him into custody. On examination it was found that the gun, a .38 Colt revolver, had five of its six chambers loaded with live ammunition with one round having a misfire impression on it.

For showing exceptional courage and heroism involving risk to his own life in this incident Detective Garda Denis Daly was awarded a Silver Scott Medal for his bravery.

Terrorist Bomb Blast, Crowe St., Dundalk, 19th December 1975.
Left to Right: Commissioner E. Garvey, Mr P. Cooney (Minister for Justice)
Mr P. S. Donegan (Minister for Defence), Supt. R. Fahy, Chief Supt. R Cotherall.
(Photo: courtesy Paul Kavanagh Collection)

As policing continued in Dundalk in increasingly tense circumstances, nobody was prepared for the terrible event which took place on 19th December 1975. Without warning, a car bomb exploded outside Kay's Tavern in Crowe Street, with devastating consequences. Tragically, two men, Jack Rooney and Hugh Watters, died as a result of the blast. Many buildings were also damaged, and unfortunately, as was the case with the 1974 Dublin and Monaghan bombings, nobody has yet been held accountable. In his Report published in December 2003, Judge Henry Barron came to the conclusion that while there was no conclusive evidence, these bombings were most likely the work of loyalist extremists.

Some months later, on Sunday morning 2nd May 1976, the body of Seamus Ludlow was found on a bye road at Mount Pleasant, a few miles north of Dundalk. He had been shot a number of times. Seamus Ludlow was 47 years of age and was employed locally as a forester. He had lived quietly with his elderly mother and other members of his family, and was not known to have had any paramilitary or political connections. Again, this murder was never solved and his family are still actively seeking answers. The Barron Report described the killing as "a random, sectarian killing of a blameless Catholic civilian by loyalist extremists". Both the bombing of Kay's Tavern and the murder of Seamus Ludlow underlined both the vulnerability of Dundalk and the surrounding district to retaliatory violence from loyalists, and the extra demands this threat placed on policing in a border district like Dundalk.

*A morning briefing in Dundalk Station (old snooker room) regarding a murder investigation, May 1976.
Seated Left to Right: Sgt Bill Burke, Gardaí Ned Connor, Brendan Cooke, Mick McGarry, Tom Molloy, Frank Clune, Mick Kilroy, Sgt. Michael Conneally, Jim Greene.
Standing Left to Right: Insp. John Courtney, Garda Patrick O'Connor, Sgt. John Igoe, Gardaí Pat Trehy, Mick Noone, Sgt. Leo Colton, Gardaí Fintan Kenny, Tom Staunton, Noel Breen.
(Photo: courtesy Paul Kavanagh Collection)*

On the night of Wednesday 5th May 1976 Garda Colm Murray, a young Garda stationed at Omeath Garda Station, was sent to do checkpoint duty at the Flagstaff Road near Omeath, a permanent Garda/Army checkpoint just over 500m from the Louth/Armagh border. At the time security had been tightened up along the border due to a few incidents which had recently taken place, the latest being the abduction and murder of Seamus Ludlow outside Dundalk a few days earlier. As he started duty, Garda Murray had no idea that later that night he would become involved in an incident that would have serious international consequences.

Garda Colm Murray.

At 10 pm a Triumph car approached the checkpoint from the North. Garda Murray questioned the driver but was dissatisfied with his answers. On shining a torch on the front passenger, the Garda saw him place a sub-machine gun at his feet and try to conceal it with a large map.

Both men, who were dressed in civilian clothes, produced British Army identification and said they must have taken a wrong turning on their return to Bessbrook Military Barracks. They also admitted that they were armed. On receiving the assistance of an Army corporal from the nearby sentry post, Garda Murray informed the two British soldiers that as they were in the Irish Republic he was detaining them. He also took possession of their weapons, a sub-machine gun, two automatic pistols and about 100 rounds of ammunition. When Sergeant Patrick McLoughlin arrived in the Omeath patrol car, Sergeant McLoughlin and Garda Murray arrested the two men under the Offences against the State Act and brought them to Omeath Garda Station for interview. At 2.30 am on Thursday 6th the men were escorted to Dundalk Garda Station.

Meanwhile, back at the checkpoint, at 2.15 am Garda Murray saw two more cars approach as if in convoy. A Hillman Avenger contained four men, and a Vauxhall Victor with two men who were dressed in civilian clothes. They all identified themselves as British soldiers, and between them the men were armed with three sub-machine guns, two automatic pistols and a sawn-off pump action shotgun, with about two hundred rounds of ammunition. They also carried a night sight, two-way radios, and maps.

Garda Murray asked the men to explain their presence in the Irish Republic. Their sergeant explained that they had been searching for two missing colleagues, and must have made a map reading error and taken a wrong turning. After further questioning by Garda Murray it emerged that the six men were a British SAS unit searching for their two comrades who had been arrested earlier. After alerting the nearby Army unit he told the SAS men that he was arresting them, and demanded that they hand over their weapons. Garda Murray reported "It was not until the Irish Army personnel made their presence felt that they eventually handed over their weapons." He also took possession of the ignition keys of both cars and locked the firearms, ammunition and equipment in the boot of the Avenger. He then reported the second detentions and sought assistance. The men were taken to Dundalk Garda Station under Garda/Army escort, where they were interviewed at length after their arrival at 4 am.

The incident created a diplomatic headache for the Government. If the soldiers were charged it would affect diplomatic relations with Britain, but neither could they appear to be released without charge. Meanwhile, as the day wore on, crowds gathered outside Dundalk Garda Station, and the media arrived. Tensions were rising, and the authorities had to act quickly to avert trouble. On the instructions of the Director of Public Prosecutions the soldiers were charged under the Firearms Act with possession of unlicensed firearms, and possession of firearms with intent to endanger life. The men were placed in a combination of marked and unmarked cars in the back yard of Dundalk Station and were taken under heavily armed escort to the Special Criminal Court in Dublin. They were later released on bail of £40,000 put up by the British Embassy and flown out of the state by helicopter.

In March 1977 the eight soldiers went on trial and were subsequently fined £100 each for possession of firearms and ammunition without firearms certificates. The guns involved had been forensically examined and were found not to have been involved in any crime under investigation in the Republic of Ireland. The incident was recorded as a map reading error, and an apology was received from the British Government.

Garda Murray was subsequently awarded a 1st Class Commendation for police work, which praised his "quiet and efficient manner in what can only be described as very delicate circumstances".

A few months later another serious incident took place in which a local Garda sergeant was shot and wounded. On 8th June 1976 Sergeant Bill Grier from Dundalk Station received a report that two men were heading towards Dundalk after being involved in a shooting incident north of the border. As the army-assisted border patrol was on their meal break, Sergeant Grier set up a checkpoint with a colleague on the old Newry Road at the New Inn junction. After a time the suspect car arrived at the checkpoint and the driver was asked to get out of the car, which he did. Because of the tight fitting jeans and jacket he was wearing the members considered him not to be carrying a firearm. As the driver then went to open the boot of the car as directed, Sergeant Grier spoke to the passenger whom he knew. When asked, the passenger got out of the car and as the sergeant was searching him, he spotted a gun sticking out of his anorak. At this stage the passenger shouted at the driver to open fire on the Gardaí. A violent struggle then ensued between the sergeant and the passenger. The sergeant pinned the passenger to the ground and endeavoured to get the gun from him. Two shots then rang out and when Sergeant Grier looked up he saw that the driver had a gun pointed at his head from ten feet away. Realising the extreme danger of the situation the sergeant ran in a zig-zag fashion towards the safety of the patrol car to summon help, but while he did so the two men continued firing after him, one shot wounding him in the right knee and another whizzing by his ear. The two assailants then made good their escape but both were later captured and sentenced to terms of imprisonment.

Sergeant Bill Grier, Silver Scott Medal, 1977.

For displaying exceptional courage and heroism involving risk of life in the execution of his duty Sergeant Bill Grier was awarded the Silver Scott Medal.

In May 1977 an event occurred just north of the Louth border with Co Armagh that to this day has been one of the most significant unresolved incidents of the troubles. This was the abduction and murder of Captain Robert Nairac who was a British Army officer attached to the army intelligence section based in the military barracks at Bessbrook, Co Armagh. While Captain Nairac was a regular army officer it seems he was also a bit of a maverick and liked to do things his own way.

Garda Search Team, Ravensdale Woods, May 1977.
Back Row Left to Right: C. McCaffrey, C. O'Gara, J. Finne, S. Dunning, L. Witherow, W. McLoughlin, M. Kelly, M. Kavanagh, E. Boyle, J. Rose, T.F. Murray, R. Roche, J. Prendergast.
Front Row: C. Murray, B.V. McCabe, T. Tully, P. McNamara, T. McGuire, P. McAuliffe, J. McCarthy, R. Duggan, H. Murtagh, R. Beehan.

On the night of 14th he visited a pub in Dromintee, South Armagh and tried to pass himself off as Danny McErlean from a republican area of Belfast As the night progressed he mixed well with the locals and even sang republican songs. However, perhaps he underestimated the locals and eventually drew strong suspicion on himself. Close to midnight he was abducted from the pub car park by a group of men after a violent struggle. He was then taken across the border to Ravensdale Park where he was interrogated for a long period of time before being killed. Because it was a cross-border incident the main Garda investigation was co-ordinated from Dundalk Garda Station. This investigation led to a conviction being secured in the Special Criminal Court in Dublin in November 1977 for the murder of Captain Nairac. After many searches over the following years to this date Captain Nairac's body has never been found.

Before the decade ended another very serious incident took place on the Louth border at Omeath where it adjoins Co Armagh at Narrow Water. Such was the seriousness of the incident it created international headlines and became known as the Narrow Water Massacre, once again drawing negative attention to North County Louth.

The events unfolded on 27th August 1979 when a British Army patrol, consisting of a Land Rover and two heavily armoured lorries carrying soldiers, was travelling towards Newry from Warrenpoint. At about 4.30 pm, as they were driving past an entrance to Narrow Water Castle at the head of Carlingford Lough and directly across the water from Omeath, a massive explosion took place, hurling the second lorry over, killing six of the soldiers and seriously injuring the remainder. Assuming they were under attack from the southern side of the border, the soldiers started firing across the water towards the Omeath area in the Republic just south of the border. Upon hearing the commotion two civilians, William Hudson and his cousin Barry Hudson, who were in Omeath running an amusement fair at the time, went down to the shore to see what was happening. Tragically, they came under fire from the British Army and as a result William Hudson was shot dead and Barry Hudson was seriously wounded. In the meantime the ambushed soldiers radioed for help, and at approximately 5 pm help arrived. An incident command point was set up beside a stone gateway on the other side of the road. No sooner had this command point been set up when another massive explosion took place destroying the wall and killing another twelve soldiers. The ambush appeared to have been meticulously planned.

Sergeant Michael Mullany, who was one of the first Gardaí to arrive at the scene, recalls *"As I stood by the Garda car a local man addressed me as follows 'Sergeant I don't think you should go down there, these fellows might start blasting'. This advice was backed up by another local who informed me that a man had been shot dead and the body of the deceased man was lying further on down the laneway.*

It was clear the Gardaí would have to deal with a very serious situation which was unfolding. With some fear and dread I decided to walk on down the lane until I had a view of the other side.

I realised it was important to make a contact, if possible. All I could do was to take hold of a white handkerchief and wave it high. To my great relief, there was an acknowledgement from the troops. This brought about an immediate reduction in tension and the Gardaí now felt secure as they set about their various tasks. Chief among them was the examination of the body on the lane way and the preservation of the scene."

As a result of these incidents eighteen British soldiers on the Northern side of the border lost their lives and one innocent civilian lost his life on the Southern side. A major cross-border investigation based in Dundalk got under way. A number of people were arrested in relation to the bombing but due to lack of evidence were later released.

This was also the same day that Lord Mountbatten, a member of the British Royal Family, was killed by a bomb blast at Mullaghmore, Co Sligo.

Before the 1970s were finished Dundalk policing was to be tested yet again with another major incident in which serious riots took place. It is referred to locally as the "Night of the Linfield Riots".

One of the most riotous nights Dundalk has ever witnessed occurred on August 30th 1979. The European Cup tie between Dundalk and the Belfast team, Linfield, was to be played in Oriel Park. Arrangements were in place for strict security as some trouble was expected, but what actually happened could not have been foreseen. Late that afternoon word was received that a group of Linfield supporters was on its way with intent to cause trouble. Sixty busloads of supporters were expected with some of them highly fuelled on alcohol.

Warning bells rang out all over the place with extra Garda reinforcements being called in on duty from the surrounding divisions. When the Linfield support arrived the buses were parked in a designated area beside the Harp Brewery, just off the Carrick Road. The supporters then made their way up the Carrick Road towards the barriers at Oriel Park. Upon arrival at the barriers a group of the supporters who were highly intoxicated wound up chanting sectarian hate songs. Due to their desire to be allowed to enter the pitch they did not create much trouble at the barriers and handed over, without much hassle, long flagpoles and anything that was considered a dangerous object.

However, after gaining entry into the grounds and going to their designated area they then proceeded to dig up clay banks and supply themselves with an arsenal of stones. As the game progressed it was like a war zone. The supporters threw stones, burned flags, climbed roofs and tore down fences. At this stage an extra three hundred Garda reinforcements had arrived from Dublin and outlying areas and this fairly strengthened the Garda position. Rioting continued and with twenty minutes to play the Linfield fans were eventually baton charged out of the grounds. They proceeded to break as many windows as possible in the area as they proceeded down the Carrick Road towards their buses. At the bottom of the Carrick Road two rows of about one hundred Gardaí had formed a human barrier, blocking them from going down the town and diverting them towards their buses. They were contained in their bus area until they boarded their transport and were eventually escorted out of the town.

By this stage ambulances had arrived and ferried the injured to the Louth Hospital. By the end of the night over a hundred people had been treated for injuries including fifty Gardaí. While not all Linfield supporters took part in riotous behaviour that night, it was nevertheless clear that the political violence of the day had also infected sport, and at the end of a troubled decade this background of violence represented a heavy burden on policing in Dundalk.

Local Crime Detective Unit, mid 1970s. Left to Right: Sgt. Dan Prenty, Supt. Dick Fahy, Gardaí Jim Boyle, Jim Greene, Tom Staunton. (Photo: courtesy Paul Kavanagh Collection)

Looking over the evidence in a local crime at Dundalk's Crime Office (left to right)—Sergeant Dan Prenty, Superintendent Dick Fahy, Garda Jim Boyle, Garda Noel Breen and Garda Tom Staunton.

*Garda senior officers in charge of Dundalk District, mid 1970s.
Left to right: Supt. Dick Fahy, Insp. P.J. Farrelly, Supt. Andy Murtagh, Insp. Brian McCabe.
(Photo: courtesy Paul Kavanagh Collection)*

Mid 1970s Checkpoint.

Chapter 5
- 1980s -

As we moved into and through the 1980s, dealing with this exceptional violence continued alongside the standard policing of a major provincial town. Serious offences of robbery with violence, false imprisonment and armed burglary continued, with Post Offices and all cash-in-transits taking big hits. While armed robberies averaged four, five, or six per year in the 1970s, in 1982 there was a sudden increase to twenty-four. The border stations of Omeath, Dromad and Hackballscross were still heavily manned with uniformed Gardaí. The thirty six official border crossings had regular checkpoints which were mostly manned by unarmed uniformed Gardaí backed up by armed units of the army from the local 27th Battalion from Aiken Barracks in Dundalk.

Shootings against unarmed uniformed Gardaí still continued. On the afternoon of 9th May 1980 a report was received of an armed robbery taking place at a jeweller's shop in Clanbrassil Street. In response, Sergeant Dan Prenty, Garda Tom Mulligan and Garda Tom Duffy set up a checkpoint at Castletown Road under the railway bridge. A brief description of the two men involved in the robbery had been circulated to the Gardaí at this stage who were also told that the getaway car had been abandoned close by. Shortly afterwards the Gardaí noticed two men of similar description strolling casually on the Castletown Road with one of them carrying a holdall. The Gardaí then gave chase in the personnel carrier driven by Garda Mulligan. Sergeant Prenty and Garda Duffy alighted from the personnel carrier and called on the men to halt. One of the men drew a revolver from his coat and fired two shots at the pursuing Gardaí. They then ran into the Ecco Road still pursued by the two Gardaí. As they ran up the Ecco Road one of the men discarded the holdall onto the roadside. The man with the gun then took aim again and fired two more shots at the Gardaí. The members took cover before continuing the chase. The two suspects then ran into a local housing area and as they did so the same gunman fired another shot at the Gardaí. Reinforcements then arrived on the scene and the area was surrounded and searched. The two gunmen were located in a coal shed at the rear of one of the houses and were arrested. A search of the coal shed yielded a handgun containing five spent rounds of ammunition plus one live one. The bag discarded in the chase was found to contain the stolen jewellery and another fully loaded revolver.

Sergeant Dan Prenty, Gold Scott Medal, 1980

For exceptional courage and heroism involving risk of life in the execution of their duty Sergeant Dan Prenty was awarded the Gold Scott Medal and Garda Tom Duffy was awarded the Silver Scott Medal.

Garda Tom Duffy, Silver Scott Medal, 1980.

From 1981 onwards more serious incidents occurred in which local Gardaí were to find themselves in challenging and dangerous situations earning them Scott Medals for their bravery.

Visit of Cardinal O'Fiaich to Dundalk Garda Station in September, 1980.
Back Row Left to Right: C. McCarron, T. Molloy, C. Murray, J. Delaney, L. Crowe, E. Boyle, S. Gettins, T. Byrne, O. Corrigan, T. Hynes, J. Finn, P. Trehy, J. Whelan, N. Smith, P. Mahony, T. Hamill, S. Scariff, B. Finnegan, K. Henry, M. Kilroy, J. Harney, E. Sheridan.
3rd Row: N. McLoughlin, J. Fahy, J. Murphy, T. Fanning, K. Harrington, M. Staunton, T. Egan, P. Ryan, L. Moran, M. McGarry, J. Coggans, G. Flynn.
2nd Row: L. Colton, D. Prenty, B. Connolly, B. Tobin, M. Driscoll, B. Cunnane, M. Kelly, T. O'Hanlon, M. Reilly, E. Connor, R. Garland, H. Murtagh, R. Roche, B. Piper, B. Grier.
1st Row: Supt. J. Keaney, Fr. F. Donnelly, Cardinal O'Fiaich, Chief Supt. Cotherall, Supt. R. Fahy, Insp. B. McCabe, Insp. T.F. Murray.
(Photo: courtesy Paul Kavanagh Collection)

On the evening of 29th November 1981 Detective Garda Terry Hynes and Detective Garda Tom Molloy were on mobile patrol in a housing estate in Dundalk with Detective Garda Molloy being the only one armed. They attempted to interview the driver of a car that appeared suspicious to them but the driver drove off at speed. The Gardaí followed the car and when they were close behind it they saw the driver take what appeared to be a submachine gun from the back seat and place it beside him while driving onto a main road and travelling at speeds of between seventy and a hundred miles per hour. After a few miles, the fleeing vehicle was involved in a collision. The driver was uninjured. He jumped from the car armed with a submachine gun and ran down a side road closely followed on foot by the two Gardaí. The gunman stopped and pointed the gun at the members who were then only a few yards away. They shouted at him to drop the gun but he fumbled desperately with the mechanism near the trigger and retreated behind a tree. The Gardaí separated and rushed the gunman from opposite directions. Their quick

Detective Garda Terry Hynes, Silver Scott Medal, 1981.

action momentarily confused him and he was overpowered and disarmed. The submachine gun had one round in the breech and seventeen rounds in the magazine while a loaded pistol and a hand grenade were found in the damaged car.

For exceptional courage and heroism involving risk of life in the execution of duty Detective Garda Terry Hynes and Detective Garda Tom Molloy were both awarded Silver Scott Medals.

Detective Garda Tom Molloy, Silver Scott Medal, 1981.

On Saturday 24th June 1983 Garda Edward Connor, Sergeant Bill Grier and Garda Michael O'Driscoll were on patrol at Seatown Place, Dundalk. Information was received by the patrol that an armed robbery was in progress at the Windmill Bar close by. Garda Connor stopped the patrol car near the front door of the bar premises. Suddenly two masked men appeared in the doorway from inside the premises. One of the men, carrying a firearm, appeared to be attempting to cock the firearm; both men warned the Gardaí to stay back or they would be shot. The men ran down Barrack Street, pursued by the Gardaí. The gunman continually pointed the gun in the direction of the pursuing Gardaí, repeating threats to shoot them. The chase continued with the gunmen entering the grounds of Realt Na Mara School and making good their escape. The money from the armed robbery was found inside the railings of the school and one of the gunmen was later arrested nearby. The second gunman was never apprehended.

For exceptional courage and heroism involving risk of life in the execution of duty Garda Edward Connor was awarded the Bronze Scott Medal.

Garda Edward Connor, Bronze Scott Medal, 1983.

On Saturday night 16th July 1983 Garda Larry Witherow and Garda Gerry O'Brien, both uniformed Gardaí, were on mobile patrol in the Dundalk area. At Marshes Upper, just south of the town, the two Gardaí stopped a container truck which had no rear lights. When they approached the front of the truck on foot, the driver and a passenger alighted from the cab. The passenger stood beside the truck and without warning fired a shot from a handgun at the two members who were eight feet away. The members dived for cover. The gunman and the driver then ran into a nearby housing estate chased by the two Gardaí. When the gunman came to a street light he took up a firing stance and fired another shot. Again, the Gardaí took cover. Undeterred, Garda O'Brien resumed the chase after the two men while Garda Witherow ran to the patrol car and contacted the local station. After running some distance, Garda O'Brien caught up with the driver, tackled him and took him into custody. The gunman escaped but was subsequently arrested.

Garda M. J. O'Brien, Silver Scott Medal, 1983.

For exceptional courage and heroism involving risk of life in the execution of duty Sergeant Gerry O'Brien was awarded the Silver Scott Medal.

Meanwhile shooting incidents against Gardaí continued along the border. At 10.40 pm on 21st July 1983 while on border patrol two local Gardaí, Willie Horgan and Joe Whelan, both based at Omeath Garda Station, set up a checkpoint at Flagstaff. Both Gardaí were in uniform and unarmed. After a time a motorbike approached them from the direction of the Long Woman's Grave, and as it slowed down, the driver did not stop but circled around the checkpoint and drove back in the direction he had come from. Closing their checkpoint the Gardaí quickly gave chase to the motorbike. In the ensuing chase they noticed a car with headlights on coming towards them. The driver of the motorbike stopped and spoke to the occupants of the car, when suddenly without warning a volley of shots came from the direction of the car. The gunfire ripped through the driver's side of the patrol car over the head of the driver and out through the rear window. Fearing for their lives and not knowing what was coming next both Gardaí jumped out of the patrol car and headed for the protection of the nearest ditches. While in the ditches they could still hear the sound of gunfire. The offending car eventually drove off. Later, upon examination of the scene one empty and one full magazine of bullets for an Armalite rifle were found. Thankfully neither of the Gardaí was injured and the following day they continued their normal Garda duties.

Still in 1983, on Tuesday 15th November Sergeant Tom Brady and Detective Garda Joe Delaney went to a dwelling house in a local housing area to interview a man who earlier that evening, armed with a .22 rifle, had stolen £40 in cash from a motorist As the two members approached the house a shot was fired from within. Garda Delaney went to the side of the house and tried to persuade the gunman to surrender. The gunman shouted, "*Go away or I'll blow your head off*". More Gardaí arrived at the scene and the gunman fired another shot.

Detective Garda Joe Delaney, Bronze Scott Medal, 1983.

Detective Garda Delaney then went to the front door of the house and engaged the gunman in conversation. At the gunman's request, a local priest was called and both he and the Garda were allowed into the house at gunpoint. They were ordered to sit at a table and further talks continued. After some persuasion from Detective Garda Delaney the gunman put down the rifle. On hearing a sudden noise at the rear of the house the gunman became visibly agitated and tried to reach for the gun. Detective Garda Delaney, using this distraction, jumped up and knocked the gun out of his reach and grabbed the weapon. The gunman was overpowered in the ensuing struggle and taken into custody. Subsequent examination of the rifle revealed that it had one live round in the breech and three more rounds in the magazine.

For exceptional courage and heroism involving risk in the execution of duty Detective Garda Joe Delaney was awarded the Bronze Scott Medal.

Sergeant Brendan Connolly, Bronze Scott Medal, 1986.

On Thursday 9th August 1984 five armed and masked men entered a house at St Alphonsus Road, Dundalk. The occupants of the house raised the alarm and the five armed men left the scene by car. The car travelled along the Avenue Road, being pursued by Detective Garda Joe Flanagan and eventually crashed at Hoey's Lane, where a number of gunshots were exchanged between Detective Garda Flanagan and the armed men. Three loaded firearms were discarded by the gunmen at Hoey's Lane. Sergeant Brendan Connolly and Garda Pat McGee, who were uniformed, unarmed and travelling in a marked patrol car, entered a local housing estate in an attempt to intercept the armed gang. As they did so they observed a masked and armed man running towards them. The gunman then raised a sawn-off shotgun and fired at the patrol car. In the ensuing struggle, both Gardaí overpowered the gunman and took him into custody. As well as the sawn-off shotgun, the gunman had also in his possession a loaded .38 revolver.

Garda Pat McGee, Bronze Scott Medal, 1983.

For exceptional courage and heroism involving risk of life in the execution of duty Sergeant Brendan Connolly and Garda Pat McGee each received the Bronze Scott Medal.

The following year another armed raid in Co Louth ended tragically with the murder of Collon based Sergeant Patrick Morrissey.

Sergeant Patrick Morrissey was born on 7th March 1936 and raised in Belturbet, Co Cavan. After completing his schooling he served in the Irish Army for a time before joining An Garda Síochána on 14th December 1960. In 1966 he became a founder member of the Garda Sub Aqua Unit and remained there until he was promoted to the rank of Sergeant in 1974. In 1976 he returned to the Sub Aqua Unit where he took charge of diving operations including the Whiddy Island disaster and the recovery of bodies that ensued from the bombing of Lord Mountbatten's boat in Mullaghmore, Co. Sligo. In 1981 he transferred to Collon Garda Station and while continuing his work as a member of An Garda Síochána he was also a volunteer with Drogheda River Rescue and Recovery service.

Sergeant Patrick Morrissey, Gold Scott Medal, 1986. (Awarded posthumously)

On 27th June 1985, as Sergeant Morrissey was about to enter Ardee Courthouse, he was told of an armed raid that had just taken place at the local employment exchange and that shots had been fired at Gardaí who had arrived at the scene. Sergeant Morrissey flagged down the patrol car and went with Garda Peter Long and Garda Brendan Flynn in pursuit of the gunmen. The three members set up a checkpoint in Tallanstown village with the intention of intercepting the getaway car. Two men riding a motor cycle approached the checkpoint and failed to stop. Recognising the two men as the armed raiders, the Gardaí then gave chase in the patrol car. At Rathbrist Cross, the Gardaí saw the two suspects running up an avenue leading to a private house. Their motor cycle had crashed into a car, seriously injuring the female driver and her three year old daughter. Garda Long and Garda Flynn attended to the scene and the injured family. Sergeant Morrissey, alone and on foot, followed the suspects. As he caught up with them, a shot was fired and he fell to the ground, seriously wounded. One of the gunmen stood over him and at point blank range shot the sergeant dead. The two gunmen then ran away. On the grim discovery of the slain sergeant a search was put into operation and the two gunmen were later arrested and taken into custody. The two gunmen were convicted by the Special Criminal Court in Dublin in December 1985 and were sentenced to death. This sentence was later commuted to forty years penal servitude.

Although Sergeant Morrissey was based in Collon and the armed robbery occurred in Ardee, the final chase and shooting ended in Dundalk Garda District, as such Sergeant Morrissey's story and memory are part of our local policing history.

For exceptional courage and heroism involving risk to life in the execution of duty the Scott Gold Medal was awarded posthumously to Sergeant Patrick Morrissey.

The 14th August 1986 was to be another riotous day in Dundalk's history. Peter Robinson, then deputy leader of the Democratic Unionist Party and later to become First Minister in the Northern Ireland Government, had been remanded to appear at Dundalk District Court charged with unlawful assembly and assault at Clontibret, Co Monaghan.

Approximately eight hundred extra Gardaí were drafted into the Dundalk area for the day, while many shopkeepers closed their premises. Armed detectives were placed on the roof of Dundalk Courthouse and barriers were erected by Gardaí to keep back the crowds arriving for the predicted trouble. Mr Robinson duly arrived with his wife and Dr. Ian Paisley amid a cavalcade of cars. The cavalcade was directed into a secure area at the Fair Green for the safety of the occupants. About two hundred of Mr Robinson's supporters paraded through the centre of the town and were marshalled into another safe zone, a short distance from the courthouse. The court case ended with the case being adjourned to the court sitting in Ballybay on 2nd October. Mr Robinson was escorted out of Dundalk via Roden Place as Gardaí in riot gear directed Mr. Robinson's supporters back to their cars through Clanbrassil Street. Petrol bombs and stones rained down on his supporters but injuries were slight. As the cavalcade of supporters were leaving town some of them had their windscreens smashed with flying missiles and more trouble flared. Again Gardaí had to baton charge and it took the full numerical strength of the Gardaí on duty to restore order. Eventually full order was restored with a number of arrests being made. Dundalk made international headlines the following day, again for all the wrong reasons. At a time when unemployment was high in the town and the statutory bodies were trying to get new enterprises into the area, occurrences like these didn't help.

A truly shocking murder took place in Dundalk on 25th April 1987. As Mary McGlinchey was bathing her two sons on a Saturday evening at her home in Dundalk, two gunmen broke in the back door of her house, ran up the stairs and fatally shot her in front of her two boys. It is generally believed that this vicious killing was part of an Irish National Liberation Army (INLA) feud. Mary had been married to Dominic Mc Glinchey and both were self-declared members of the INLA and very heavily involved in its structure and activities. At the time of Mary's death Dominic Mc Glinchey was serving time in Portlaoise Prison. He was eventually released from prison in 1993, but more tragedy was yet to follow. On 10th February 1994 Dominic Mc Glinchey was shot dead in front of his son at a phone box on the outskirts of Drogheda. Although major investigations were carried out into both killings, the crimes remain unsolved.

Before the end of the 1980s another very serious cross-border incident took place involving the murder of two senior Royal Ulster Constabulary officers shortly after they crossed the border into Northern Ireland after attending a security meeting at Dundalk Garda Station. The incident gained international headlines and was later to lead to one of the biggest enquiries in the State with allegations of a mole being present in Dundalk Garda Station.

On 20th March 1989 Chief Superintendent Harry Breen and Superintendent Bob Buchanan of the RUC attended a cross-border security conference at Dundalk Garda Station. Both of them travelled in Superintendent Buchanan's private car and parked outside the station at about 2 pm. The two policemen were unarmed and wore civilian attire. As pre-planned, the meeting began shortly after 2 pm and finished at about 3.15 pm. At this stage both men returned to their private car and headed back towards Northern Ireland travelling on the main Dundalk/Belfast road. Approximately two miles north of Dundalk they turned left and went up the Edenappa Road towards Jonesboro, which lies just across the border. Shortly after crossing the border they drove into an armed ambush and were shot dead by four masked and armed men wearing battle fatigues. The shooting occurred at about 3.40 pm and was later claimed by the South Armagh Brigade of the Provisional IRA. Naturally enough the question then begged to be asked how could such a well-planned and successfully executed ambush be arranged in such a short span of time, and how did the IRA know which road the two policemen would take heading northwards? Different theories and allegations arose regarding the shootings, but unfortunately one of those allegations was that there was a mole in Dundalk Garda Station who was passing information to the IRA. This allegation was hotly disputed by all Garda and civilian staff working in the Station at the time.

Different investigations were carried out both north and south of the border into the shootings but these were inconclusive. Eventually the Irish Government commissioned Judge Peter Corry, a retired Canadian Supreme Court judge, to carry out an independent investigation and to report his findings. In his concluding report Judge Corry stated that after carefully considering all the relevant factors, the intelligence reports and the Fulton statement (allegations of Garda collusion by double agent Kevin Fulton), he concluded that the documents revealed evidence that, if accepted, could be found to constitute collusion.

On the basis of Judge Corry's findings, the Government decided to set up a tribunal which was to be a full judicial enquiry into all matters surrounding the killings. In July 2006 Judge Peter Smithwick began his investigation and on 7th June 2011 the public hearings began in Dublin. Two and a half years later, on 3rd December 2013, Judge Smithwick's findings were published. One of his main findings was that while unable to find direct evidence of collusion, he believed that on the "balance of probability" there was collusion between Gardaí from Dundalk Station and the Provisional IRA in the murder of the two senior policemen. There is no doubt that this finding cast a shadow and a doubt over all personnel working in the station at the time. While the findings of the Smithwick Tribunal were respected they were not totally accepted by the Garda members who worked out of Dundalk station during these perilous times.

Chapter 6
- 1990s onwards -

Garda Statue, Ice House Hill Park, Dundalk, August 1995.
Erected by Martin Naughton in memory of his father with an accompanying plaque which reads:
"In Memory of Garda Martin Naughton and all members of the Garda Síochána who served in Dundalk since the foundation of the State. August 1995

Sergeant Michael Mullany's Retirement on the 8th April 1995
Left to right: Superintendent M. Staunton, Sergeant Michael Mullany,
Assistant Commissioner Barney Curran, Inspector John Grant, Sergeant Tom Deery,
Garda Noel Scully (Dated 5/4/95)

Entering into the 1990s, paramilitary crime appeared to be easing, and ceasefire talks were beginning in Northern Ireland. With a degree of awareness, the normal standard policing of a major provincial town like Dundalk was beginning to take shape again, but without warning a further atrocity was to take place. Tom Oliver was a highly respected farmer who lived at Riverstown, Dundalk on the Cooley Peninsula with his wife and seven children. On the evening of 18th July 1991 he went to tend to his stock and never returned. The following day his body was found near Belleek in Co Fermanagh having been shot many times. This murder elicited untold sympathy and support for the Oliver family nationally. Unfortunately nobody has been made accountable for this killing, and this investigation is still ongoing.

On 31st August 1994, a unilateral ceasefire was declared by the Provisional IRA, which resulted in a scaling down of Garda resources along the border. However by 1996 a new crisis arrived and with it all thirty six border crossings had to be manned again as the dreaded Bovine Spongiform Encephalopathy (BSE) disease was found in animals in England, and for the protection of Irish meat products the border had to be sealed. Approximately one hundred and fifty extra personnel were transferred from down the country to the Dundalk district alone. Confrontations on these checkpoints were minimal and Gardaí met with great cooperation. The operation may have been expensive for the state but the results were one hundred per cent successful.

Garda P. O'Donoghue, BSE Checkpoint, 1996.

1997 was the 75th anniversary of the foundation of the State and also of An Garda Síochána. On 9th October Dundalk Gardaí celebrated the occasion by having an open day at the Garda Station. The event started with an interdenominational service in the Friary Church at 2 pm, and a reception for invited guests and dignitaries was later held at the Garda station at 3 pm. Then from 4 pm the Garda Station doors were opened to the public until 9 pm. The afternoon included tours of the station, incorporating displays of crime detection, exhibits, fingerprinting, a tour of the communications systems and many more examples of police work. The cell area seemed to have a fascinating curiosity for many, especially the children. Outside was a display of Garda vehicles and at 5.30 pm a recital from the Garda Band was enjoyed by all. In retrospect the open day celebrations went extremely well. Local members came in on their own free time and put in tremendous effort resulting in a great sense of pride around the place. Approximately three thousand people visited the station, mostly families. About one thousand children were fingerprinted and proudly went home with their exhibits. There was great interaction with the public.

Members on duty at Dundalk Garda Station, 11th September 1997.

Back Row Left to Right: P. O'Connor, G. O'Connor, J. Sheridan, E. Boyle, G. Murray, E. Sheridan, C. Byrne, M. Hallinan.
3rd Row: G. McArdle, E. Rice, T. Hynes, A. Costello, J. O'Keeffe, P. Tobin, T. Jones, P. O'Donoghue, T. Fox, M. Keating, N. Horgan, C. Kealy, H. Murtagh, B. Mohan, S. Gettins.
2nd Row: T. Boyle, J. McMahon, N. McGowan, R. Flynn, C. Manning, C. Deloughery, K Keogh, S. Keane, M. Beggy, P. O'Hanlon, C. McGuinness, A McArdle, M. Malone, J. Corrigan. (clerical staff)
Front Row: T. Mulpeter, Insp. T. Brady, Supt. M. Staunton, Insp. P. McGee, L. McGinn, J. Fahy.

Dundalk Garda Station decorated for 75th Anniversary.

Parade Leaders from Friary Church 75th Anniversary.
Left to right: J. O'Keefe, V. Jackson, C. Deloughery, J. McMahon, C. Keely, R. Flynn.
(Photo: Courtesy Paul Kavanagh Collection)

*Garda Band Recital 75th Anniversary.
(Photo: Courtesy Paul Kavanagh Collection)*

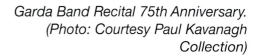

*Garda Band Recital 75th Anniversary.
(Photo: Courtesy Paul Kavanagh Collection)*

*Old friends Ronny Roslyn and retired Garda Joe Gaffney enjoying a chat at 75th Anniversary.
(Photo: Courtesy Paul Kavanagh Collection)*

D/Garda G. Murray fingerprinting young lady 75th celebrations.

D/Garda J. Ryan fingerprinting young lady 75th celebrations.

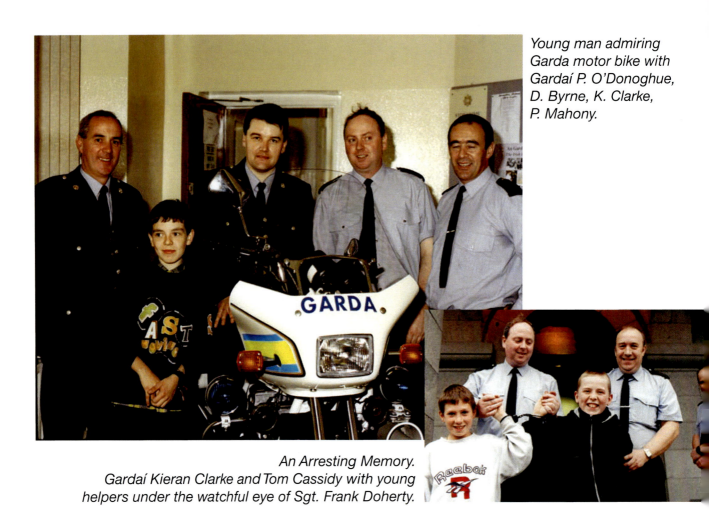

Young man admiring Garda motor bike with Gardaí P. O'Donoghue, D. Byrne, K. Clarke, P. Mahony.

*An Arresting Memory.
Gardaí Kieran Clarke and Tom Cassidy with young helpers under the watchful eye of Sgt. Frank Doherty.*

Gardaí enjoying 75th Anniversary.
Left to Right: D. Shannon, V. Jackson, T. Mulpeter, P. Mahoney, H. Murtagh, T. Duffy, A. Costello, M. Beggy, S. Keane, H. Downey, N. McGowan.

From recollection, there was a deafening silence in the station the following morning after the noise from the hustle and bustle of the previous evening. Members were exchanging stories of events from the evening before with smiles and a good sense of humour. One member recalled an "*ordinary decent criminal*" calling to the Station to know what was going on. On being told of the occasion being an open day he enquired if he could bring his wife and family up. Being assured there was no problem, he went and brought them. Needless to say he conducted his own personal tour without any help and was most helpful if any other member of the public had a query!

Equine Visitors at Station.
Left to Right: B. Kealy, P. O'Donoghue, J. Lynch, D. Prenty, J. O'Hare, J. Keogh, J. McGuire, G O'Brien.

Even after the 1994 Provisional IRA ceasefire the shadow of the previous years of violence was still to remain. Families of the "Disappeared" were still asking questions and looking for the remains of their loved ones to be returned. Eventually as part of the peace process an Independent Commission for the Location of Victims' Remains was established in 1999. The body was set up by the British and Irish Governments to obtain information in strict confidence to help locate the remains of a number of people who had disappeared during the troubles. This International Commission was headed by Sir Kenneth Bloomfield, former head of the Civil Service in Northern Ireland, and ex-Tánaiste John Wilson. As part of this same peace process the IRA admitted to the murder of nine of the disappeared and to burying them at secret locations. The bodies of two of the disappeared turned up in north Co Louth.

Patrol outside Garda Station, October 1997.
Left to Right: Garda A. Costello, Sgt T. Mulpeter.

Gardaí from Louth/Meath Division on duty at Slane Concert, 1999.
Left to Right: O. Keegan, G. McGovern, J. Mulvanny, B. Keane (Dundalk), A. Donohoe (Dundalk), D. Monaghan

On the morning of 28th May 1999 Gardaí at Dundalk Garda Station received information that a coffin with a body in it lay at a corner of Faughart Cemetery, a few miles north of Dundalk. The information also said the coffin was above ground and contained the body of Eamonn Molloy. This was the first of the disappeared to be returned to his family.

On the following day, 29th May, as a result of further information being received, a search party of Gardaí were sent to Templetown Beach, Carlingford, to dig for the remains of Jean McConville. Jean McConville was a widowed mother of ten young children who had been abducted from her home in Belfast on 7th December 1972. She was never to return home and through the peace process information was given that her body was buried at Templetown Beach.

Garda Commissioner Pat Byrne's visit to Templetown Beach, Dundalk, 1999.
Left to right: Garda C. Kealy, Sgt. F. Doherty, Insp. P. McGee,
Assistant Commissioner P. O'Toole, Garda A. Donohoe, Commissioner P. Byrne, Garda P. Mc Govern, Garda R. Sheehy, Sgt. J. Kilcoyne, Garda P. O'Hanlon, D/Garda K. Reidy, Chief Supt. M. Finnegan.
Front Row: D/Garda E. Sheridan, Garda P. O'Donoghue.

Search Site Templetown Beach, 1999.

As this was a high profile case the international media had gathered at Templetown and strict security precautions had to be put in place. However, a search that was planned to last for only a few days lasted for most of the summer with no result. The frustration of the McConville family was plain to be seen, especially for the family members who spent every day there waiting for their mother's remains to be found and wondering if the next spadeful of sand would reveal some clue. Being in close proximity the Garda search team members got to know the McConville family quite well and often shared their elevenses with them while explaining to them how the dig was going. Sometimes on a Saturday night when work was finished both parties would meet in Lilly Finnegan's local pub, have a brief discussion on the week's work and then a full discussion on the coming football matches over the weekend. Each county was well represented in these serious discussions.

What impressed the Garda members, while working on the site, was the kind and caring nature of the people from the locality, and how they supported the McConville family during this unnatural and difficult time. They made sure they wanted for nothing even from the point of view of turning up in strong numbers in the evening time if the rosary was being said or if any other religious service was taking place.

By 17th July 1999 approximately 200,000 metric tonnes of sand had been excavated and sifted through and still there was no breakthrough in the search. The dig was eventually called off causing great disappointment to the family but at this stage every avenue had been explored with the information that had been received. The following year on 2nd May the search was resumed due to fresh information being received and a new area was dug up and sifted through, but unfortunately this new area revealed no evidence and the dig eventually concluded on 18th May 2000.

On 26th August 2003, a man out walking his dog came across human remains at the nearby Shelling Hill Beach and finally these remains were proven to be those of Jean McConville. It appears that the remains eventually became exposed due to the tide and the shifting of the sands. The beach certainly held its secret for over thirty years but was now bringing closure to this part of the Jean McConville story. There was never much doubt regarding the information that was being given regarding the whereabouts of Jean McConville's body. It appears to have been genuine and given in good faith, but memory can also play tricks over a period of thirty years.

Jean McConville was eventually laid to rest at the Holy Trinity Cemetery in Lisburn Co Antrim following Requiem Mass at Saint Paul's Church in West Belfast on 1st November 2003.

On 12th December 2000 a massive security operation was put in place when the President of the USA, Bill Clinton, visited Dundalk with his family. The town centre was sanitised and not a stone was left unturned. Approximately sixty thousand people turned up for this momentous occasion which passed without incident. Everything about the event was run with extreme precision, with strict care and attention being given to even the smallest possibility of a breach of security. Months of planning went into the operation and information was passed on only on a "need to know" basis with over eight hundred Gardaí on duty covering before, during and after the visit. The Presidential helicopters were based at the local military barracks but could not be used due to the foggy weather conditions and

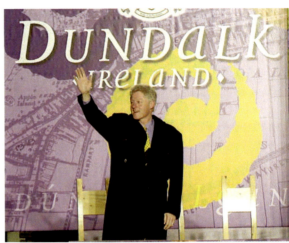

President Bill Clinton's visit to Dundalk on the 12th December 2000 (Photo: courtesy Arthur Kinahan)

therefore the decision was made for the presidential convoy to come down the new M1 motorway which at the time was completed but not fully open to the general public. The convoy duly arrived into town driving up through Barrack Street, Jocelyn Street, Francis Street and turning right into Earl Street before finally stopping outside of R Q O'Neill's shop (now Pamela Scott's). The President and his family arrived at 9 pm and left at approximately 10 pm after receiving a very warm welcome from the townspeople. The event certainly put Dundalk on the world stage again but more positively this time and from a policing point of view it was a major success. In his memoirs President Clinton referred to his visit by commenting, "*On 11th December Hillary, Chelsea and I flew to Ireland, the land of my ancestors and scene of so much of the peacemaking I had done. We stopped off in Dublin to see Bertie Ahern and went to Dundalk near the border for a massive rally in a city that was once the hotbed of IRA activity and is now a force for peace. The streets were bright with Christmas lights and a large crowd cheered wildly as they sang 'Danny Boy' to me. Seamus Heaney once said of William Butler Yeats, 'His intent was to clear a space in the mind and in the world for the miraculous'. I thank the Irish for clearing that space in the mind and for the miracle of peace.*"

On 21st February 2001 foot-and-mouth disease was found in animals in Great Britain and as a result on 22nd February a ministerial order came from Government to set up checkpoints and cordon off our border with Northern Ireland, thus putting into action what was to become one of the biggest security operations ever undertaken by the state. Again in north County Louth with its twenty nine miles of border and thirty six border crossings very strict security measures were put into place with the thirty six crossings being funnelled into nineteen static checkpoints with every vehicle that passed through being checked.

On 28th February an outbreak of the disease was found just north of the border in Meigh, Co Armagh, and on 23rd March a similar outbreak was found in Proleek, Ravensdale, north Co Louth. This resulted in a three kilometre checkpoint zone being placed around the infected area, followed by a ten kilometre exclusion zone. This required a further fourteen checkpoints to be manned along with the nineteen static checkpoints already operating on the border. At the same time another ministerial directive was issued stating that all of County Louth was to be sealed off and every vehicle going in or out was to be screened. This left a total of sixty seven checkpoints to be manned on a twenty four hour basis with up on eight hundred extra Gardaí being transferred into County Louth alone to perform this duty.

The checkpoints were operated with the assistance of the Department of Agriculture, the Irish Army and the Civil Defence force. Risk assessments were carried out on each checkpoint with the general safety and welfare of the members being taken into consideration. Coinciding with the duty of manning the checkpoints a serious criminal investigation was also taking place with regard to the introduction of the disease into the State.

The whole operation was very successful, again aided by the good will and cooperation that came from the general public. After four weeks the checkpoints monitoring movement in and out of County Louth were lifted and by mid-July the static checkpoints in the north of the county were replaced with mobile patrols. The crisis had been averted and normality eventually returned.

As we continued into 2001 a further tragedy occurred in the Dundalk area resulting in the loss of another Garda life. Detective Garda Desmond Dixon was based in the specialised units section at Garda Headquarters in Dublin. On Thursday 15th November 2001 he was on duty in the Dundalk Garda area driving an unmarked Garda car along the southern link road travelling in the direction of Dublin, when at about 7.25 pm a car travelling on the wrong side of the road and coming towards him from the opposite direction crashed into him. As a result of the accident and the injuries received Detective Garda Dixon was later pronounced dead at the Louth County Hospital. Originally from Raheny in Dublin, Desmond was survived by his wife and three young children. Prior to serving at Garda Headquarters, Detective Garda Desmond Dixon had also served at Store Street, Clontarf and Howth Garda Stations.

Detective Garda Desmond (Des) Dixon. Accidentally killed on duty, 15th November 2001.

By the year 2002 times were not just as troubled as previous decades but the unknown challenge of police work and danger still lurked in the background. On 15th January 2003 Garda Gerard Collins and Garda Darren Kirwan were on mobile patrol in the Dundalk area when they got a call around 3.15 am reporting that there was a man sitting on the Castletown Bridge threatening to jump into the river. As the Gardaí approached the man shouted at them to keep away or he would jump. Then without any warning he jumped into the freezing waters. On seeing that the man was being dragged into the central channel of the river that feeds into Dundalk Bay and realising he was in serious danger of drowning, the two Gardaí jumped into the river and swam towards the spot where they had last seen him. On reaching him they found him in a very distressed state but managed to hold onto him with great difficulty as they battled against the freezing temperature and the strong current. Eventually they succeeded in bringing him to the river bank and from there he was taken to hospital.

Garda Gerard Collins, Bronze Scott Medal, 2005

For showing exceptional courage and heroism involving risk to life in the execution of their duty Garda Gerard Collins and Garda Darren Kirwan were each awarded the Bronze Scott Medal.

Garda Darren Kirwan, Bronze Scott Medal, 2005.

*Local Gardaí returning from security duty at President Bush's visit to Ireland, June 2004.
Back Row Left to Right: P. Dunne, D. Fanning, J. Mangan, P.J. Galvin, J. Minnock.
Middle Row: M. Clarke, C. Harrison, A. M. Monaghan, A. Hanlon, J. Whelan, R. Sheehy.
Front Row: P. O'Donoghue, J. Brady, D O'Donnell.*

Having retired from the Garda Force in 2005 after thirty three years' service I assumed that I had seen and heard most of the problems and grief associated with policing in a busy and often controversial place like Dundalk. I was wrong, for there was more tragedy yet to follow. Nothing could have prepared me for the phone call I received on the evening of 25th January 2013 informing me that an ex-colleague, Detective Garda Adrian Donohoe, had been shot dead in an armed robbery at Lordship Credit Union. I thought how cruel it was that a murder like this should occur after the years of violence seemed to have passed. It made me wonder if the legacy of the gun ever leaves an area.

Detective Garda Donohoe was born on 14th January 1972. He was raised on the family farm at Kilnaleck, Co. Cavan along with his three brothers and two sisters. He joined An Garda Síochána in 1994 and after training was posted to Dundalk Station. He later married Caroline (a fellow Garda) and together they had two children. Later in his career he was appointed to the rank of detective. In carrying out his duties as a Garda he was known for his ability to help people and steer them out of trouble. He was held in very high regard as a contributor to his local community, Lordship. On the GAA front he played with St Patrick's GAA of Lordship and won a senior championship medal with them in 2003.

Detective Garda Adrian Donohoe, Gold Scott Medal, 2016. (Awarded posthumously)

Detective Garda Joe Ryan, Silver Scott Medal, 2016.

On Friday evening 25th January 2013 Detective Garda Adrian Donohoe was on duty with his colleague Detective Garda Joe Ryan. Both were on a cash escort duty with Detective Garda Ryan being the driver. It was a routine patrol. At 9.30 pm the Garda car entered the car park of Lordship Credit Union with another car that had accompanied them from a different Credit Union. Suddenly a car crossed the road and blocked the entrance to the Credit Union. As Detective Garda Donohoe got out of the car to investigate what was happening a masked raider came from behind and shot him. Detective Garda Donohoe died almost instantly. Before Detective Garda Ryan realised what had happened he was held at gunpoint by three masked and armed raiders.

The raiders then broke into the car belonging to the Credit Union staff and made off with €7,000 in cash and assorted cheques, leaving a much larger sum behind them. The five man gang then fled the scene, taking with them the keys of the patrol car. The emergency services pronounced Detective Garda Donohoe dead shortly after their arrival. While one man has been convicted for the capital murder of Detective Garda Adrian Donohoe, the investigation is still ongoing.

For exceptional courage and bravery involving the loss of life in the execution of duty Detective Garda Adrian Donohoe was posthumously awarded the Gold Scott Medal.

For showing exceptional courage and bravery on the occasion his colleague Detective Garda Joe Ryan was awarded the Silver Scott Medal.

Sadly, within three years, another tragedy occurred that was to rock the local Garda force yet again. A local Garda, Garda Tony Golden, lost his life as he carried out his duty aiding a victim of domestic violence in Omeath, Co Louth.

Garda Tony Golden was born on the 20th January 1979. Originally from Culleens, Ballina, Co Mayo, he married a local girl, Nicola O'Sullivan, and they lived in Blackrock with their three young children. Garda Golden was regarded as a good community policeman and had been very popular and highly respected in the locality. He was based as a Garda in Omeath, Co Louth, and had completed ten years' service. Tragically he was to lose his life while protecting a member of his district as he had done so many times in the past.

Garda Tony Golden, Gold Scott Medal 2017 (Awarded posthumously)

On Sunday evening 11th October 2015, as a result of a complaint of domestic abuse, Garda Golden went in the Garda patrol car with the female victim and her father to a housing estate in Omeath. The purpose of the visit was to protect the victim while she retrieved her belongings, as she was moving away from her abusive partner. The victim's father was directed by Garda Golden to stay in the patrol car for his own safety. As Garda Golden and the woman entered the house the male occupant challenged them and then shot Garda Golden five times. Following this, he then shot his partner a number of times before turning the gun on himself and taking his own life. Local Garda Gary O'Callaghan was first to respond and provide assistance, but it was too late for Garda Golden. Miraculously, the young woman survived.

Garda Gary O'Callaghan, Silver Scott Medal, 2017.

For exceptional courage and bravery involving the loss of life in the execution of duty Garda Tony Golden was posthumously awarded the Gold Scott Medal.

For his bravery and presence of mind on the occasion Garda Gary O'Callaghan was awarded the Silver Scott Medal.

Chapter 7
- History of Dundalk Garda Station -

While researching the policing history of Dundalk and North Louth, I naturally enough found myself drawn into researching the history and origins of the fine building that is now the present Dundalk Garda Station. As this building was both the administrative centre and Governor's residence of the former prison, I found that it and the general prison area held some fascinating history. Thinking that my investigations would end there, I then found myself drawn into researching the previous jail sites in Dundalk and their linkage with policing and courts.

According to Tempest's Annual (1972), 1686 appears to be the first record of a jail in Dundalk, when a Mr. Justice Nugent found a very full prison. *"He tried near three score persons; some were condemned and most discharged after having been whipt or burned in the hand"*. This jail *was described as "The old castle called Castleynrooty otherwise known as Hyndes Castle"*. It is believed to have been situated at the junction of Church Street and Clanbrassil Street.

Having discussed this research with local historian Harold O'Sullivan (RIP), he believed that the next established jail was situated in Clanbrassil Street on the site that is now the "Dublin House" licensed premises. Oliver Plunkett, Roman Catholic Archbishop of Armagh, is believed to have been incarcerated in this jail while awaiting trial. There may have been other prison sites at that time but I cannot find verification of them. However, it is widely believed that prior to the building of Crowe Street Jail all imprisonment took place in the Clanbrassil Street/Church Street area.

It is not known exactly when Crowe Street jail was built other than it was before 1793, in which year the Governor was Denis Fitzpatrick and the hangman was one Brian Carrol who lived in Squeeze Gut Alley (Defenders Row) and was commonly known as "Brian-a-Muck". Brian-a-Muck was reputed to have approached his job with a callous humour. The Governor, Denis Fitzpatrick was regarded as being a *"very humane and considerate person"* to the prisoners under his control. This jail stood on the site of the present Town Hall and it is here that three men were hanged in 1816 for the burning of Wild Goose Lodge near Reaghstown, Co. Louth in which eight persons died, including one infant. The bodies of the hanged men were left hanging publicly for several days, while the bodies of the other fifteen men convicted and hanged for the same crime were gibbeted in North and Mid Louth. While the evidence for the convictions was believed to be very dubious, the authorities wanted results.

A new jail, to be added on to the old jail at Crowe Street, was proposed by the Grand Jury in 1816 and completed by 1820 at a cost of £16,000. The old jail building was reserved for debtors and the new jail for felons. For its time it was regarded as having been well advanced, having its own kitchen, laundry, hospital, schoolroom and exercise yard. Water was provided by a treadmill in the yard. Male prisoners were employed at breaking stones while female prisoners were employed at spinning, sewing and knitting. By 1823 the total number of prisoners was forty six. It even had an underground passage to the present Courthouse, which remained in place until 1931, when it was partly demolished and closed up to make room for the new County Council offices. It was rediscovered circa 1985 when the Courthouse was being refurbished and to this day it is being used as a passage way to the lower ground cells.

However, by 1837 overcrowding was creating serious problems with ninety prisoners for thirty one cells, and although overcrowding was always a problem the prison continued to function.

The Jail, Dundalk.
(Photo: Courtesy The Lawrence Collection, Dublin National Library)

Due to the overcrowding and poor conditions in the jail in Crowe Street, the Grand Jury decided that a new prison needed to be built. A three acre site was acquired at an area formerly known as Gallows Hill, now known as the Crescent. The architect selected for its construction was John Neville who was also the county surveyor for Louth.

As Dundalk was the county town, John Neville was instructed to design and build a prison that would be architecturally pleasing and prestigiously apt in addition to serving its primary purpose as a jail. The building started in 1844 with an initial costing of £18,000. By the end of 1849 the work was well under way, and early in 1850 Neville requested permission to remove "the drop" (the gallows) from the front of Crowe Street Prison so that it might be incorporated in the new building. This never materialised, and before its final destruction it was used for the execution of James Kirk and Patrick McCooey which took place on July 31st, 1852. The hanging took place outside the Crowe Street Jail where the present Town Hall stands. It is reported that a large crowd from around the county came to witness this event, which was the last public hanging to take place in Dundalk.

The building John Neville designed is described in the North Leinster Architectural Archive: "*An Italianate building of severe grandeur. Grey granite ashlar in the main block flanked by rubble walls with cut stone arches; well sited above a sloping semi-circular green. The walls screen two long rubble-built gaol buildings (radiating from the central block), whose quoined chimneys are visible from the street below. The main building is of square shape with projecting corner blocks. Two storeys over a concealed basement. The principal elevation is of five bays, the centre three recessed, screened by a tall single storey loggia and crowned by a square two-storey tower with a pyramidal roof. Square-headed windows to the ground floor; round headed above. A deep band of vermiculated rustication provides a base for the building*".

A clearer description of the interior of the building comes from *The Civil Engineer and Architect's Journal, Vol. XVII (1853)* in which it states "*The prison is designed in the separate system, and*

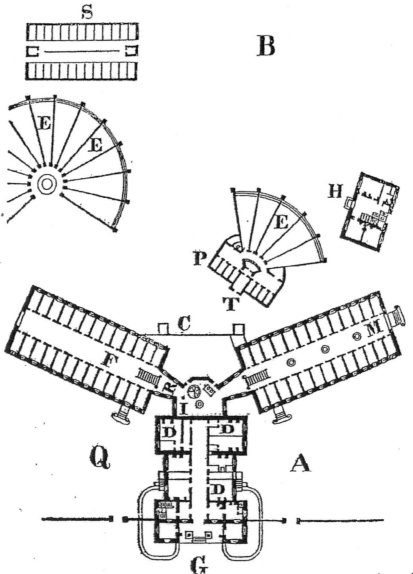

G, entrance to offices; D D, debtors' prison; A, garden where the debtors take exercise; I, inspector's hall; F, female prison; M, male prison; C, large coal stores, capable of holding 60 tons, which can often be procured in Dundalk at a cheap rate when taken in large quantities; P, pump, worked by a crank and prison labour; T, tank, placed on a tower whence the prison is plentifully supplied with water; E E E, exercising yards for prisoners; H, hospital; S, stone-breakers' sheds; B, back-gate and depot for stones; Q, quarry, now filled up. The Governor's house, chapel, and school-room, are placed over the building G D D; and the kitchen and offices, punishment cells, &c., underneath.

Accommodation.

	M.	F.		M.	F.
Wards,	3	1	Worksheds,	24	—
Yards, on separate system,	18 for all.		Kitchen,	one.	
Day Rooms, for Pauper Debtors; also used for Lunatics,	1	1	Store Rooms,	4	1
Solitary Cells,	2	2	Laundry,	one.	
Single Cells, not less than 9 feet long, 6 feet wide, and 8 feet high = 432 cubic feet,	83	21	Drying Room, not fitted up,	one.	
			Lavatories—There is a basin in each cell at water-pipe, for washing.		
Single Cells of larger size,	2	1	Baths,	1	1
Rooms for Master and Mistress Debtors,	2	1	Privies,	eight.	
Do.	2	1	Water-closets,	seven.	
Hospital Rooms,	4	1	Do. in cells,	107	
Chapels on separate system,	one.		Reception Rooms or cells,	4	5
School Rooms—Stalls in Chapel used for this purpose.			Pumps and Wells—Two pumps connected with cranks, and one single-hand pump; two wells connected.		
Workshops—prisoners generally work in cells.			Tell-tale Clock,	one.	

Dundalk Gaol layout.
(Photo: Courtesy National Archive, Forty-third Report of the Inspectors General on the General state of Prisons of Ireland, 1864,)

consists at present of a central building and two radiating wings. In the entrance building apartments are provided for the governor and turnkeys; it also contains governor's office, waiting room, visitors'-room, board-room, local inspector's office, matron's apartments, and accommodation for master debtors. The chapel connects the entrance building with the prison, and is so constructed as to contain 168 separate sittings if required hereafter. Two doors from the inspection hall admit the prisoners, and on the opposite side a door is provided for the officers and chaplain to enter the front building. The basement storey contains reception and punishment cells, baths, laundry, drying-room, kitchen and dishing room, coal, clothes and provision stores, and also 20 extra cells. There are at present 126 ordinary cells; 13 ft. x 7ft. x 9ft. 6in. arched at the top, 104 of them having oak flooring and are fitted up, heated, and ventilated in every way in accordance with the provisions of the separate system. There are 24 exercising yards…. Stone-breaking sheds are also constructed at the rear… Every arrangement (has been) made for an extension at any time of the 270 separate cells".

The work was completed in 1854 at a cost of £23,000. Tradition has it that the excess cost rendered the builder bankrupt and as such he became the first inmate as an "undischarged bankrupt". In that year seventy prisoners were transferred from Crowe Street to the new prison. In 1875 Patrick Hartigan became the first prisoner to escape having scaled the 20 foot wall. His escape was short lived as he was captured shortly afterwards.

In 1915 the jail was taken over by the British Military, and in 1917 the Governor's House was adapted by a local voluntary aid detachment (Red Cross) as a twenty bed hospital for sick and wounded British soldiers.

During the War of Independence the jail was used as a prison for political prisoners and on one occasion they engaged in a hunger strike led by the famous Kerry Republican Austin Stack. During the Civil War the prison was used by both the Pro-Treaty and Anti-Treaty sides depending on which side was in control at the time.

On the 27th July 1922 at 7.15 am a well planned and executed attack by Anti-Treaty forces was made on the jail. A mine exploded against the wall on the Ardee Road side creating a major breach in the wall and resulting in one hundred and five prisoners escaping, including Frank Aiken. Aiken's forces regrouped and on 14th August 1922 successfully launched an all-out attack on the military barrack, which was captured with some loss of life. The captured soldiers were then marched as prisoners to the jail but due to the inadequacy of the accommodation, a number of the prisoners were handcuffed to the railings fronting the jail.

On the 13th January 1923 at 8 am by direction of the Provisional Government, three prisoners, Thomas McKeown, John McNulty and Thomas Murray were executed by firing squad in the prison yard. After the execution their bodies were buried in the prison yard; the exact location is unknown. It was not until October 1924 that their bodies were exhumed and handed over to their respective families.

When the Civil War came to an end the jail reverted to civil use and officially closed down in 1931.

During the Emergency in the 1940s the Governor's Residence of the block was used as headquarters of the local security forces. These forces known as the LDF (Local Defence Forces) were trained by Gardaí as part-time police and military auxiliaries.

In January 1946 the Gardaí moved from Anne Street Station to the Governor's Residence and established a new headquarters there. Over a period of time the two cell blocks fell into decay and remained that way for a number of years. Eventually they were refurbished with the original female block now housing the County Archives and the male block the new Oriel Centre.

Exterior Photo of Dundalk Male Prison wing, prior to refurbishment.

Celtic Cross graffitti on a cell wall in Dundalk Prison, prior to refurbishment.

Interior Photo of Dundalk Male Prison wing, prior to refurbishment.

Interior Photo of Dundalk Male Prison wing, prior to refurbishment.

Chapter 8
- Local Garda Commissioners -

North County Louth was to contribute two Garda Commissioners to the force. Michael John Wymes was born on 22nd December 1907 at Castletown Road, Dundalk. He came from a policing background with Michael (senior), his father, being an RIC policeman based at Anne Street Police Station. His father was also listed as a subscriber to the building fund of Saint Nicholas's Church in Dundalk from 18th February 1905 to 1st March 1908. At the time of the 1916 Easter Rising he was one of the two RIC sergeants who monitored the movements of the local volunteers on their journey to join in the Rising in Dublin. As a result of the events that took place on this journey (mentioned earlier in Chapter 2), Sergeant Wymes, along with ninety other policemen from all over Ireland, were presented with certificates of honour, for what was termed *"their conspicuous service in the suppression of the rebellion of 1916"*. The presentation took place on Thursday 17th May 1917 at the RIC depot in the Phoenix Park, Dublin. Along with the certificate of honour each of the policemen was given £5 in scrip of the war loan. Sergeant Wymes was later promoted to the rank of Head Constable and retired on full pension on 16th September 1920.

Following a policing tradition his son Michael John Wymes later joined An Garda Síochána and rose to the highest rank in the force, becoming Commissioner of the Gardaí from September 1968 to January 1973. Having served in different stations throughout the country he established himself as a talented crime detector which eventually led to him taking charge of C3 (the security section at Garda Headquarters) in the Phoenix Park, Dublin before becoming Commissioner. Regarded as being a quiet and sometimes shy man he was held in high esteem by the Government of the time and regarded as a safe pair of hands. He led the Gardaí through a difficult transitional period of policing in Ireland from the late 1960s to the early 1970s.

Commissioner Michael Wymes.
(Photo: courtesy Garda Archives)

After Commissioner Wymes resigned, his position was taken over by another Co Louth man, Patrick Malone, a native of Riverstown, on the Cooley Peninsula north of Dundalk. Patrick Malone joined An Garda Síochána in 1931 and in the earlier part of his career he served in most of the Garda Divisions outside of Dublin. Eventually he was promoted to the role of Assistant Commissioner in 1971. In 1972 he was appointed as Deputy Commissioner and in January 1973 he became Garda Commissioner. After forty one years' service, he resigned on 1st September 1975. Recognised as a conscientious administrator he was also regarded as a person who possessed a keen sense of responsibility and resourcefulness. In 1974 as Commissioner he played a major role in the establishment of the Garda museum / archives.

Commissioner Patrick Malone.
(Photo: courtesy Garda Archives)

A Border Beat - Policing in Dundalk

Conclusion

State policing, whether by the Royal Irish Constabulary or by An Garda Síochána, has been a feature of life in Dundalk, as elsewhere in Ireland, for almost two hundred years. While much of the policing carried out by the RIC was for the common good, it was nevertheless true that this force was also the strong arm of British rule and a landowning elite. RIC men, who were themselves very often farmers' sons, can hardly have felt comfortable at having to assist in evicting tenant farmers like Lawrence Crawley and his family at Kilcroney.

From 1922, Irish people at last had the opportunity to police their own independent state. The Civic Guard, very soon renamed An Garda Síochána, was unarmed because its members were policing with the consent of the people and with their moral support. It was a new force, but some continuity of policing traditions can be seen in the career of a man like Thomas Kinahan from Dromiskin, who was a detective in the G Squad in the Dublin Metropolitan Police early in his career, and continued as a detective in An Garda Síochána when the two forces amalgamated in 1925. The Wymes family also represents continuity between the old and new. Sergeant Michael Wymes (RIC), from Anne Street Police Station, was given the task of monitoring the movements of volunteers from Dundalk as they set out to join the Rising in Dublin in 1916. His son, also Michael, who was an eight year old boy at the time, would later become Commissioner of An Garda Síochána, the future police force of the independent state which those same volunteers were fighting to establish.

Policing methods have changed extensively since the early days, especially since the establishment of An Garda Síochána. From originally policing their districts on foot or on bicycles, and with little or no means of communication outside their barracks, the contrast with modern policing which makes full use of forensic science and IT is stark indeed. Nevertheless, Gardaí have successfully policed the Dundalk area, a task which became both much different and considerably more difficult from the 1970s, when Dundalk ceased to be like any other large provincial Irish town.

In the days of the RIC, the Louth-Armagh county boundary was no more significant in terms of policing than the Louth-Meath boundary. With independence came the partition of Ireland, and the Louth-Armagh boundary became an international border which has been in place throughout the existence of An Garda Síochána. Border patrolling is a unique policing experience. In peaceful times a border presents its own challenges, but in troubled times like the decades following 1970 it takes on a totally different dimension. Experienced Gardaí have referred to the border as being a multi-cultural area to police, where Gardaí encounter a northern culture, a southern culture, and a distinct border culture which is located uncomfortably between them.

Due to its geographical position, Dundalk Garda District has often been a very challenging and even dangerous area to serve in. Notwithstanding that, like most members I found it a rewarding place to serve the public and I have many good memories along with some sad ones. The greater unpredictability of daily policing compared with many other centres in the country made unusual demands on those who served in the area, and often prompted truly courageous responses. A significant number of members who have served in Dundalk have been awarded the Scott Medal for bravery, and within Dundalk District five Gardaí have lost their lives in the course of duty. It is to the memory of those deceased members I dedicate this book.

Addendum

The following document has been researched and kindly given to me by Trevor Patterson, Secretary of Dundalk Select Vestry (Saint Nicholas's Church of Ireland, Dundalk). It lists police, prison, excise and coastguard personnel as recorded by name and occupation in the registers of St Nicholas's Parish Church, usually as the fathers of baptised or buried children. The first year listed is the earliest they were thus mentioned.

Police 1816-1834

The names listed here include men who served in the temporary Peace Preservation Force (PPF) from 1816, and in the permanent County Constabulary established in 1822. The Town Sergeant may possibly have been a local appointment independent of either the PPF or the Constabulary.

Sergt Knowles   [Sergt Police]   1816
Hugh Kelly   [Police]   1816
Thomas Hunter   [Police]
… Haycock   [Constable]   1816
John Murphy   [Police]   1816
Samuel Keys   [Police]   1816
John Forbes   [Police]   1816
… Wigan   [Police]   1816
George Cluxton   [Police]   1817
Henry Forbes   [Police]   1817. A Henry Forbes was buried on 31-8-1820
Joseph Hanna   [Police]   1817;   also reference to   … Hanna   [Paymaster, Police]   1817
… Coles [Police] 1818
David Moore   [Police]   1818
Thomas Keys   [Police]   1818
Terence Mara   [Police]   1818
Henry Cunningham   [Police]   1818
Robert Sinclair   [Police]   1818;   also reference to … Sinclair   [Police] in 1817
Andrew Walker   [Police]   1818;   also reference to … Walker   [Police] in 1817
Isaac McDaniel   [Police]   1818
Robert Hunter   [Police]   1819
George McCalvey   [Police]   1819
Abel Jackson   [Police]   1819
Hector McDonald   [Police]   1819
John Brierton   [late of Police]   1819
James Cole   [Louth Police]   1819
William Woods   [Town Sergt]   1819, 1821, 1825. A William Woods of Dundalk was buried on 24.5.1837.
William Armstrong [Chief Constable]   1821, 1825, 1826. A William Armstrong of Dundalk was buried on 29.9.1832.

James Kiniday [Constable]   1822, 1824
William McGragh [Constable]   1823, 1824, 1825, 1827
Charles Whittager [Constable]   1823; [as Town Sergeant]   buried 2.6.1827
Edward Jenkins [Capt. Police]   1826, 1828, 1830
James Harvey [Police Man]   1826
William Howell [Police]   1827
John Barrett [Police]   1827, 1828, 1831
Thomas Thompson [Police]   1833
Ross Reid [Police] 1833, 1835. Referenced again without occupation 1836 and 1839.
George Scott   [Police]   1833
… Kilfoyle   [Police]   1833
… Foster   [Police]   1833
William Johnston   [Police]   1834
Thomas Hust   [Police]   buried 17.4.1834

Prison Officers

Denis Fitzpatrick [the Gaoler]   1803, 1810. Referenced without occupation 1805 and 1807.
John Crowe   [Jail]   baptismal record 19.8.1823.   A John Crowe of Dundalk was buried 17.10.1823.
Patrick Ross   [Schoolmaster, Gaol]   1824
Robert McDowell   [Turnkey]   1827
James Clerk   [Turnkey]   1828

Excise Officers

*Richard Jones   [Surveyor of Excise]   1796
*John Moran [Gauger] 1799, 1802 [A gauger measured the contents of casks of liquor for taxation]
*George Terril   [Gauger]   1800
*James Forde   [late Collector of this Port]   buried 17.3.1803
John Dawson [Sergt Excise] 1808 [Marriage Register]
Mr Sweetman   [Revenue]   buried 15.10.1814
David Patterson [Revenue] 1816
John Reilly   [Custom House]   1816, 1817
Mr Rowan   [Gauger]   1817]
Thomas Parkinson [Revenue Officer] 1818
John Roberts   [Gauger]   1820, 1826, 1828
Robert Marks   [Tidewaiter]   1824, 1826, 1829   [A tidewaiter boarded ships in harbour to enforce customs regulations]
Thomas Huntley   [Gauger]   1824
Richard Jennings   [Gauger]   1826 [Marriage Register]
Frederick Middleton   [Revenue]   1827
William Hunt   [Revenue]   1828
George Howell   [Excise Officer]   1831

George Wilkinson   [Excise]   1831, 1833
William Middleton   [Excise]   1829, 1832
Henry McClintock of Dundalk   [1843]   [Collector of Customs at the Port of Dundalk – memorial stone inscription, St Nicholas's Churchyard]

Irish Preservative Water Guard (Coastguard)

The Irish Preservative Water Guard was established from 1809, and in Co Louth from 1820/21. Blackrock was one of two additional stations established in Co Louth in 1822.

Thomas Hodges   [Watter Guards]   1824
Charles Lambert   [Watter Guards]   1825
Francis Reid   [Watter Guards]   1825
William Stannis   [Watter Guards]   1825 [Marriage Register]
William Wright   [Watter Guards]   1827
Edward Handfield   [Captn Watter Guards]   1834

*Recorded in the No 1 Register of St Nicholas's Church which holds data from 1727 to 1803.
All other references are from the No 3 Register of St Nicholas's Church [1803 to 1844]

Bibliography

Abbott, Richard, *Police Casualties in Ireland 1919-1922* (Mercier Press 2000)
Allen, Gregory, *The Garda Síochána: Policing Independent Ireland 1922-82* (Gill & Macmillan 1999)
Bennett, Richard, *The Black And Tans* (Barnes and Noble Books 1995)
Brady, Conor, *Guardians of the Peace* (Prendeville Publishing 1974)
De Búrca, Marcus, *The Curious Career of Sub-Inspector Thomas McCarthy,* (Tipperary Historical Journal 1988)
Gavin, Joseph and O'Sullivan, Harold, *Dundalk a Military History* (Dundalgan Press 1987)
Herlihy, Jim, *The Royal Irish Constabulary* (Four Courts Press, 1999)
McGarry, Fearghal, *Eoin O'Duffy, A Self-Made Hero* (Oxford University Press 2005)
McNiffe, Liam, *A History of the Garda Síochána* (Wolfhound Press 1997)
O'Brien, Gerard, *An Garda Síochána and the Scott Medal* (Four Courts Press 2008)
O'Neill, Pádraig, *History of Knockbridge* (Patrick Myres producer and printer 1994)
O'Sullivan, Donal J, *The Irish Constabularies 1822-1922* (Brandon 1999)
Whitmarsh, Victor, *Dundalk in the Emergency* (Victor Whitmarsh publisher, 1980)

Official Reports
Corry Collusion Enquiry Report 7th October 2003
Barron Report 11th December 2003
Smithwick Report 3rd December 2013

Newspapers
Dundalk Democrat
Irish Times
The Argus
Irish Independent

Journals
Garda News
Garda Review
Iris an Garda
Tempest's Annuals (1940, 1972)

Sources
Garda Síochána Museum/Archives Dublin
Louth County Library
National Archives Dublin